Baseball *in* LONG BEACH

Baseball
— in —
LONG BEACH

Bob Keisser

THE History PRESS

Published by The History Press
Charleston, SC 29403
www.historypress.net

Unless otherwise noted, all images appear courtesy of the *Press-Telegram* archives.

First published 2013

Manufactured in the United States

ISBN 978.1.60949.996.9

Library of Congress CIP data applied for.

Notice: The information in this book is true and complete to the best of our knowledge. It is offered without guarantee on the part of the author or The History Press. The author and The History Press disclaim all liability in connection with the use of this book.

CONTENTS

INTRODUCTION AND ACKNOWLEDGEMENTS

There's nothing easy about writing a book, but it certainly helps to have access to a century's worth of history.

Like every sportswriter, I thought about writing books long before getting around to it. The idea of doing one on Long Beach's storied baseball history began in the mid-2000s, when former Poly star Tony Gwynn was closing in on three thousand hits and a short time later the Hall of Fame, and in 2008 when Blair Field celebrated its fiftieth anniversary.

I spent sixteen years at the *Los Angeles Herald-Examiner* and was there when the newspaper closed. Nine months later, *Long Beach Press-Telegram* sports editor Jim McCormack hired me in 1990. He told me I'd come to respect Long Beach's history, but I had no idea then how much it would impact me.

The *Press-Telegram* has been covering the local baseball scene since before Recreation Park opened in 1924. Frank T. Blair was the former sports editor who kept the embers of building a stadium here warm for three decades. I realized the true scope of baseball here when I started seriously researching the book and got so caught up in plowing through stories, anecdotes and clips that I didn't start the writing part early enough.

Hopefully, readers will be as fascinated as I am about the early days of baseball in Long Beach and the many people who made their mark as Major Leaguers, local legends, coaches, scouts and Dirtbags.

The final chapter of the book is a registry of area players at nine high schools—the seven in the Moore League and two Catholic schools—and Long Beach State and Long Beach City College. There are two additional parts of the registry noting those who reached the majors from greater Long Beach schools—Gahr, Norwalk, Los Alamitos and Cerritos College among others—as well as Major Leaguers who were born in the area but didn't play prep or college ball at area schools. If I had one goal, it was to mention as many people as possible, and at least on that count, I think I cleared the fence.

Thanking the people who contributed to this book could be a book by itself. I'm indebted to Tony Gwynn, Bobby Grich, Harry Minor, Dave Snow, John Herbold, the late Duke Snider and two dozen others for their time. The people who helped me make a career in newspapers are all Major Leaguers, too—Joe Dojcsak, Nick Beck, Bud Furillo, Allan Malamud, Rick Arthur, Jim McCormack, Jim Buzinski and my colleague for an amazing thirty-eight years, Doug Krikorian. It would not have been possible without access to past stories by two dozen *Press-Telegram* writers and columnists—from Krikorian, the lead columnist for more than two decades; to Billy Witz, one of the *P-T*'s most prolific writers; and to Gordie Verrell, who covered the Dirtbags as comprehensively as he did the Dodgers. I also want to thank former executive editor Rich Archbold for the courtesy of the *P-T* photo library. It also could not have been done without the support of my magnificent son Chris Keisser, who gets a save for always providing support and enthusiasm.

Chapter 1

A PARK, A FIELD, A LEGACY

Long Beach had a helluva year in 1924.

By year's end, the population of Long Beach had increased by more than 15 percent from the previous twelve months thanks to the oil boom in Signal Hill. A bond issue of $3.5 million was approved to dredge the outer harbor to create the Long Beach Port.

The city council approved building its own municipal gas plant. The Long Beach Central Bank was organized. Building flourished, with the opening or construction of the Egyptian Theatre on Fourth Street, the Bank of Italy on Third Street, the Press-Telegram building on Pine Avenue and the Heartwell Building.

Joe Jost's opened its doors on Anaheim Street as a restaurant and then added a barbershop, pool tables and a poker parlor. Haircuts and eight-ball eventually gave way to its current status as dispenser of beer, community and goodwill.

And in 1924, four baseball fields at Recreation Park were proposed, authorized and completed, Long Beach's own Fields of Dreams.

It isn't an overstatement to say the Red Park's impact has been as prolific as anything in Long Beach. How many baseball games have been played at Rec and its successor, Blair Field, since 1924? One hundred thousand? How many young men and women in Southern California with a baseball dream stepped on the field at Park and Tenth? One million?

If you ask the men who have been around Long Beach baseball for any significant part of the last ninety years, they will claim that every

Blair Field.

young man in Southern California between the ages of fourteen and twenty-two who played high school, American Legion, Connie Mack or collegiate baseball have played a game at Rec Park (1924–1957) or Blair Field (1958–2013).

Those original baseball fields were built to accommodate baseball and softball, and the main field at the Northwest corner had its own one-thousand-seat shell of a grandstand. Baseball was just one part of Rec Park. It also included a golf course that became known as "duffer's paradise" in its early years; it is now Recreation Golf Course, which has eighteen- and nine-hole courses and is considered the busiest golf course in the nation.

Tall oaks and eucalyptus trees were planted on the facility, supplementing those already on the land, and they now surround and shroud the park like emissaries. Now there's Rec's successor, Blair Field, the Joe Rodgers softball stadium, the Billie Jean King Tennis Center and a lawn bowling facility.

But the baseball fields were always the hub of the facility. A well-worn hub. They were used so often that the infield grass on all four fields was shredded within five years, leading the city to remove what was left of the grass and turn all four fields into dirt infields.

"There was a lot of good baseball played at Recreation Park," Harry Minor, a Wilson High grad and professional player, coach, manager and scout, Long Beach's all-in-one icon, said. "There wasn't a single ball player in Long Beach who didn't play at Rec Park. We had plenty of ball fields in town, but Rec Park was the signature park. If you loved baseball, it's where you wanted to play."

The common touch was the kids, but professionals came to town to use Rec Park as well. The park officially opened on March 14, 1924, with a game between the Pacific Coast League (PCL) Los Angeles Angels and

Major League Chicago Cubs, both owned by William Wrigley. The Angels briefly made Rec Park their spring training home that year.

It didn't take long for baseball people to start mentioning Rec Park as a possible home for a minor league franchise.

"The City of Long Beach is building a handsome municipally-owned baseball plant for the Angels to do their training in," wrote the *Sporting News* in its February 7, 1924 edition. "Long Beach has aspirations to enter the Coast League ranks some day. That city can build baseball parks because the royalties from oil wells are piling up a big surplus in its treasury."

A year later, the PCL's Salt Lake City Bees made Rec Park its fall home, followed by Seattle in 1927 and Denver of the Western League in 1928. In 1925, Bees owner Frank Lane scheduled the first two home series of the regular season at Rec, against the Portland and Vernon franchises, because of inclement weather in Utah.

Lane was bullish on Rec. "Your baseball park is as well-equipped and laid out as any minor league plan I have seen," he said in the January 29, 1925 edition of the *Sporting News*. But no team ever took any strong steps to move to Rec or make any gesture to finance an expansion of the park.

Rec was the spring training home in 1933 for the New York Giants, featuring Mel Ott, Bill Terry, Carl Hubbell and Long Beach Poly product Jack Salveson, and on March 13, they played a free exhibition game against the PCL's Hollywood Stars. The Stars included a former Major League catcher named Johnny Bassler, twenty-year-old outfielder Vince DiMaggio and Fred Haney, who almost three decades later would be the first G.M. of the American League Los Angeles Angels.

No other Major League teams used Rec Park thereafter, perhaps because of the Giants' harrowing stories of enduring the March 10, 1933 earthquake a few days earlier.

The Giants were staying at the Robinson Hotel and most of the players were inside when it hit. Otis Brannon suffered an injury when his leg got caught between a door and wall trying to get out of the hotel. Pitcher Vance Page dove out of a window to escape.

"I leaped through where a front window had been and followed the mob to the beach front," Giants manager Ossie Vitt said in the *Sporting News* on March 23, 1933. "I was right at the edge of the water. Then someone yelled tidal wave and we all headed away from the beach."

When the ground stopped moving, Vitt summoned the team bus, and the team took off for high ground—in this case, Signal Hill, which is where the Stars were training, who were just as spooked by the quake as the Giants.

The last official flirtation with Rec as a home for pro baseball was in 1935 when Branch Rickey, then the general manager of the St. Louis Cardinals, visited Southern California to meet with PCL owners about starting a new minor league. The league would include San Diego, Santa Barbara, Riverside, Fullerton, Santa Monica and Long Beach, and those cities would also serve as spring training camps for Major League teams.

The idea was not well received by owners of the PCL's Angels, who viewed it as competition for fans. The last prewar spring training visit was by the Philadelphia A's in 1940, for one game between Connie Mack's team and an all-star Long Beach squad.

Thereafter, Rec Park was used by city kids, high schools, youth and semipro teams 90 percent of the time, serving as the seed for a parade of CIF champs and future Major Leaguers. In the winter, it was a regular stop on the barnstorming circuit.

There were other parks in town. Two years before Rec Park opened, Shell Stadium was built atop Signal Hill by the eponymous oil company, a direct result of the discovery of oil in the city. The Shell Oilers—featuring a mix of local ballplayers, major and minor leagues who made Southern California their off-season home and Shell employees who worked the derricks—became the facility's resident team, getting most of its use during the winters in the '20s when the Oilers were a team in the California Winter League.

Long Beach today is known for having more parks per square foot than any other city, and many of them featured a ball field—Heartwell in Lakewood, Houghton Park and Whaley Park. But Rec was always the go-to public park.

It hosted barnstorming games from the '20s to the '50s, including teams headed by Bob Feller, Satchel Paige and its own Bob Lemon. "Every winter there would be a local team made up of major and minor league players who lived and grew up in Long Beach, and they'd play whatever all-star team was barnstorming through Southern California," said Minor. "Some of those barnstorming games were like traveling all-star teams."

By the late '40s, Rec was in disrepair. The Parks and Recreation Department was having trouble keeping grass thriving anywhere. The stands were damaged and rickety. "Over time, it became a bit of a disgrace," said Minor. "There wasn't a single blade of grass anywhere. They would hose down the field to control the dirt."

Recreation Park might have continued to fade if not for the persistence of one man, Frank T. Blair, the sports editor of the *Press-Telegram* from 1921 to 1953, who attended that first official game at Rec Park back in 1924.

Blair Field.

Blair was a huge baseball fan and by the '40s had personally seen the first generation of Major League ballplayers from Long Beach. He was convinced Long Beach was at a point where it deserved a stadium, not just four dirt fields.

"Frank got behind the idea that the city needed a ballpark worthy of the baseball being played here," said Minor.

He believed Long Beach was a good candidate for a minor league franchise and began urging the city to get behind building a stadium. Why not? The PCL, which was a AA minor league through 1945 and AAA thereafter, had franchises in Los Angeles and Hollywood and once fielded teams in Vernon and Venice. The California League was an A League with teams in Anaheim, Bakersfield, Stockton, Santa Barbara, San Bernardino, Riverside and Ventura.

"When Long Beach gets its Class A baseball park, it will be of a caliber to attract major or minor league clubs for spring training, but the immediate and chief beneficiaries of the modern diamond layout will be the (college) and high school squads, local semipro nines…and Legion teams during the summer season," Blair wrote in a March 9, 1949, column.

"(Frank) was the nicest sports writer I ever met," Lemon told the *P-T* before a baseball function in town in February of 1956. "He was always supporting whatever kind of baseball that was being played here."

Chuck Stevens, the Poly–to–St. Louis Browns–to–PCL star, said all of the local Major Leaguers supported Blair's idea. Lemon went as far as donating money for an initial proposal for a park and approached the Cleveland Indians about putting a minor league team in Long Beach, should a stadium ever materialize.

"Everyone always said Long Beach was the only major city in the country that didn't have a decent baseball park," Rod Ballard, Long Beach's chief of the city's recreation department sports programs, said in a May 1958 *Press-Telegram* article. "And it got a bit embarrassing, too, since we produced so many top ballplayers and this was the off-season headquarters for so many baseball people."

"Through the years the Long Beach schools have had a real appreciation of the friendly attitude of Frank Blair toward our sports program," said Harry Moore, the longtime Long Beach Unified Sports director whose name graces the Moore League, in the same article. "He always had a sympathetic understanding of our problems."

Blair died on January 11, 1953, from a heart attack suffered a week earlier. Soon after, the city began putting his idea into action.

In February 1956, the citizens approved a $4.9 million bond issue for a new park. On May 15, 1956, it officially named Blair Field in Frank's honor. "When the city finally decided to build the stadium," the late *Press-Telegram* sports editor John Dixon said, "the city council didn't forget who had always advocated it."

"Long Beach was a conservative town. It was hesitant to name a street or a park after anyone, living or dead," said Stevens. "That perhaps tells you what people thought of Frank."

In November 1956, the old wooden grandstand was demolished. Construction of the new field and grandstand was completed in late 1957, and locker rooms and other internal enhancements came in early 1958.

Blair Field did not evolve as Blair originally proposed, proving once again that timing is everything. The city was hopeful of attracting a minor league team, but by 1957, there were rumors that a Major League team was moving to Los Angeles.

The Brooklyn Dodgers became the Los Angeles Dodgers and the New York Giants became the San Francisco Giants in 1958, and the Los Angeles Angels (Spokane), Hollywood Stars (Salt Lake City) and San Francisco Seals (Phoenix) of the PCL immediately relocated.

With that, the idea of a minor league team at Blair came to a quick end. Frank Blair likely would have been OK with that. His emphasis always was on youth ball.

Blair Field was scheduled to open on March 7 for a game between Poly and Montebello, but it was rained out. The first "official" game at Blair was reset for April 15, 1958, between Long Beach State and Long Beach City College. The 49ers, led by Roger Hull, beat Joe Hicks's Vikings, 14–6. Ironically, it was the same day that the Dodgers played their first game as the L.A. Dodgers, versus the Giants in San Francisco.

But the actual first game was on April 11, 1958, between Long Beach Poly and Huntington Beach High. Poly needed a park for a makeup game and talked the city into opening Blair as a shakedown for the "official" opening.

"We weren't even supposed to be playing there," legendary Poly coach John Herbold said. "It was a hush-hush deal. We didn't have a place to play, and Rod (Ballard) felt sorry for us. He said go ahead and play at Blair, but keep it quiet.

Mayor Ray Kealer throws out the first ball at the official first game at Blair Field, alongside Nelson Blair (left), Frank Blair's son, former major leaguer Chuck Stevens and Long Beach State head coach John McConnell.

"Well, the word got out, I guess; there was a picture on the front page of the *Press-Telegram* the next day."

Poly's Gordon Nelson threw the first pitch, and Poly won the game 3–1 with future Major Leaguer Tommie Sisk getting the win in relief.

The official dedication was held at the May 10 game between the 49ers and San Diego State. Mayor Ray Kealer threw out the first pitch with Nelson Blair, the son of Frank Blair; Chuck Stevens; and Long Beach State coach John McConnell alongside.

Two pro games in 1958 drew as much notice as the prep and college games and showed what Blair had in mind. On October 12, local promoter Bill Feistner arranged an all-star game between local Major Leaguers and an all-star team of other Major Leaguers, many of them Dodgers. It truly was a showcase for several generations of local ballplayers.

Lemon coached the Long Beach team that featured Lou Berberet, Rocky Bridges, Bud Daley, Joe Amalfitano, Joe Duhem, Jack Graham, Bill Wilson and Harry Minor. In the stands were older stars—Eddie Bockman, Frank Gabler, Jack Graham, Jack Rothrock, Jack Salveson, Vern Stephens, Lee Stine and Bobby Sturgeon. Ron Fairly, the former Jordan star who broke in with the Dodgers in 1958, played for the opposing team.

On December 26, the Dodgers winter team played the Long Beach Rockets semipro team, with the home team winning 8–7 behind a home run by longtime PCL star and Poly product Duhem. The Dodgers squad included Willie Davis, Don Drysdale, Fairly, Dick Gray, Charlie Neal, Ed Roebuck and John Roseboro. Dorsey High grad Sparky Anderson, who played for the Phillies in 1958, also played.

On April 9, 1961, the Dodgers played an exhibition game against the expansion L.A. Angels' Dallas–Fort Worth farm team that drew 4,250. The Dodgers won 5–3, with aging Don Newcombe, bidding for a roster spot on the team, pitching for the Dodgers against Dallas and a young shortstop named Jim Fregosi.

In 1966, the Chicago Cubs, featuring future Hall of Famers Leo Durocher, Ernie Banks, Billy Williams and Fergie Jenkins, used Blair as a spring training site and hosted eight games there, including one against the Giants and Willie Mays. The Major League Angels and Indians played an exhibition in Blair in 1967.

Since then, Blair has been home to Moore League baseball, CIF playoff games, American Legion, Connie Mack and Pony League play, barnstorming winter games, the Area Code Games and hundreds of youth clinics.

A 1993 picture of the Dirtbags stretching at Blair Field, the first season that the team started referring to themselves as the Dirtbags.

In 1993, it became the permanent home for Long Beach State. The association with Blair began in 1992 when the city agreed to a $1.4 million renovation that included new seats, a new roof, upgraded lighting and a modern drainage system. The 49ers became Blair's first full-time tenant in 1993 and, on February 5, hosted and beat Cal, 12–3.

By 1993, the team was already affectionately known as the Dirtbags. The team got its nickname in 1989 when it was forced to practice on whatever dusty field it could find, and dirt became as much a part of the players' uniforms as the team name.

Long Beach head coach Dave Snow, school and city officials negotiated the contract because the blossoming program needed a home and the park had begun to show its age. "We had already been to the College World Series, but we wouldn't have reached the stature we had if we hadn't played in Blair." Snow said. "It was a real home, and we eventually got the chance to host NCAA regionals."

In 1998, Baseball America ranked Blair as one of the top fifteen college baseball stadiums in the nation. Under Snow, the Dirtbags went to the College World Series four times, and the Dirtbags hosted a NCAA regional four times under Snow's successor, Mike Weathers. It took just two decades for the program to become a primary source of talent for the Major Leagues.

In the last three seasons (2010–12), there were more Dirtbags on Major League rosters than any other university.

Starting in 1996, Blair also accommodated several different independent minor league teams that were more carpetbaggers than tenants, though they did open the way for beer to be sold at Blair.

A park may be a park, but in terms of the number of players that played at Rec or Blair on the way to the Major Leagues, they were as productive as any of the oil wells that helped shape Long Beach.

Chapter 2

THE SWEETEST LEMON

Robert Granville Lemon's first baseball game was notable because he was ill with colic. His mother, Ruth, swaddled her newborn son in blankets and took him to the San Bernardino Opera House to watch a large manually operated baseball scoreboard for the first game of the 1920 World Series between the Cleveland Indians and Brooklyn Dodgers.

"I think I was six days old and I got the colic," Bob Lemon said in an interview with Rich Roberts of the *Press-Telegram* on May 10, 1970. "It was two weeks," Ruth said. "Earl (his dad) and I were big baseball fans."

Call it terrific foreshadowing that the Indians won that game, 3–1, and Bob Lemon would spend his entire Major League career with Cleveland.

"I brought up a winner," Ruth said in that same interview. "I don't know if it's my fault, but I always say I grew the biggest Lemon there ever was."

Certainly, he was the most popular Lemon in Long Beach. Bob Lemon remains the most iconic baseball figure in Long Beach's long history with the game, not just for his status as a Hall of Fame player but because of his lifetime link to Long Beach and an engaging, friendly personality. He became a youth star before he was a teenager, went to Wilson High and won the first-ever California Interscholastic Federation (CIF) for the Southern Section (SS) Player of the Year award in 1938, as a shortstop, and signed with Cleveland a few weeks later.

He spent all fifteen seasons of his career with the Indians, but as a pitcher, winning 207 games and being elected to the Hall of Fame in 1976. He spent eight seasons as a Major League manager, including three stints and one World Series

Bob Lemon in his Wilson High days. He was an infielder for the Bruins and was the CIF-Southern Section player of the year, the first ever selected by the division.

title with George Steinbrenner's fractious Yankees, and spent the rest of his life with a lot of the same friends that he had first met in Long Beach as a kid.

Earl and Ruth Lemon moved from San Bernardino to Long Beach before their son was two and never left. Neither did Bob. Long Beach was the perfect place for a congenial, rambunctious youngster who spent every day on the local fields, including ground zero for baseball in town, Recreation Park.

"All summer we played from daylight till dark," Lemon said in the May 10, 1970 interview. "Anytime mom and pop weren't working, they were at the ballgame. Both of them worked hard and we didn't have a lot, but anytime I needed a glove or a ball it seemed like we could always get it."

He did his chores, albeit unusually. "He had a method," his mom said. Ruth was a pastry chef, and Earl, who turned down a chance to play for Portland in the Pacific Coast League for financial reasons, ran a gas station. "We told him he'd have to mow the lawn and take care of the yard because we had to work. So he'd sit on the porch and wait till the other kids came by. They'd say, 'Let's go play ball,' and he'd say, 'I can't go till I get the lawn done.' So they would help him."

Those kids and Lemon formed the core of Long Beach's first fleet of baseball stars. Jack Graham, Vern Stephens and Bobby Sturgeon all went on to play in the majors. The kids usually congregated at Lemon's home or his dad's gas station on Fourth Street.

Red Meairs, who would go on to become a popular player and manager of the perennial softball national champion Long Beach Nitehawks team, was perhaps his closest friend as a kid scuffling around Wilson and Recreation Park.

"We grew up together," said Meairs. "He lived on Tenth and Ximeno, I lived on Tenth and Belmont, and we'd play baseball most every day we could.

"When we got older, we played every Sunday on the Long Beach Rockets [a semipro team], and after the game we'd all come back to Pop Lemon's gas station [Termino and Fourth] and have a beer or a soft drink. Mostly a beer."

Stephens helped Poly to a CIF title in 1936. Two years later, Wilson fell short of the title game, but Lemon was named Player of the Year. The nucleus of the '38 Wilson team would get to the CIF title game in 1939 and win it in 1940.

"Bob was a great player," said Harry Minor, the Wilson star whose career in baseball lasted sixty-five years. Minor was a Wilson star in the '40s and started his pro career in baseball in 1947, as a player, manager and most notably one of the greatest scouts in baseball history. "There were a lot of good players, but Bob was an exceptional hitter and fielder.

"I think I was 14 when I met Lem. My Legion coach pushed me into the lineup. He was about as down-to-earth person as you'd ever want to meet. He was so nonchalant about everything.

"Al Johnson played a role in his development because Bob used to show up late for school and he'd get all these demerits. Al finally told Bob he couldn't rely on him and he started Red ahead of him. That's all it took for Bob to get serious. He and Red became great friends as a result."

A shot of Bob Lemon early in his career, circa 1948. *Bob Keisser collection.*

Lemon went from Recreation Park to the Indians organization almost overnight, signing a contract with the Indians and hopping on a bus to their minor league team.

"I had a lot of time to think about what was going to happen to me during that trip," Lemon said to Tracy Ringolsby of the

Press-Telegram on January 12, 1978. "But I never imagined how many good things were ahead of me."

He played in Oswego, New York, for the Indians C league team in the Canadian-American League, hitting .312 with seven home runs as an outfielder before a late-season move to Springfield, Ohio, in the Mid-Atlantic League.

The next four years were spent moving up the Indians' minor league system, getting two late-season call-ups to the majors, the first in 1941 and then in 1942, after hitting twenty-one home runs and driving in eighty RBIs with the Indians' International League team in Baltimore. He spent the next three years in the military. It was during his three-year stint in the navy, mostly stationed in Los Alamitos and playing a lot of military baseball, that the seeds of moving to the mound were planted.

Lemon's hard throws to first as an infielder always had a bit of a downward tail. It was during those wartime games that Yankees catcher Bill Dickey and Birdie Tebbetts, another catcher who would go on to manage, said he should consider pitching because of that natural sinker.

Before long, Red Sox icons Johnny Pesky and Ted Williams were just as impressed by Lemon's pitching and were telling colleagues he had Major League ability. "Lemon is among the toughest pitchers I ever faced," Williams said.

"Lem had short, stubby fingers and could not throw what the rest of us called a straight ball," said another Major Leaguer from Long Beach, Chuck Stevens, to Ringolsby in 1978. "Almost everything he threw was a sinker. There were very few balls hit in the air off him."

"I didn't have to work at it," Lemon told the *Press-Telegram*'s Dick Zehms in September 1954. "The slider was a natural. I didn't even know I had it until the fellas started complaining about the tricks the ball was doing when I was pitching batting practice."

When he returned to the Indians in 1946, he was the Opening Day center fielder and made a diving catch of a line drive that he turned into a double play to save Bob Feller's shutout against the White Sox. He was in the outfield because his position, third base, was held secure by Ken Keltner. It was then that manager Lou Boudreau took the suggestions, assigned Lemon to work with Indians pitcher Mel Harder and turned him into a Hall of Fame pitcher.

A lot of people besides Dickey and Tebbetts talked about Lem becoming a pitcher—Joe Angel, the Indians scout who signed him; old-timer and Long Beach resident George Caster; and Hall of Fame Major League manager

Bill McKechnie. Lemon was so stubborn about it that when he did pitch, he refused to use the standard pitcher's toe plate that guarded the top of his cleats.

He made thirty-two appearances in 1946, five of them starts, and finished the year with a 4–5 record but a shiny 2.45 earned run average. He was a control pitcher whose natural sinker, not an asset when he was a third baseman, had batters hammering the pitch into the ground.

"He had a great arm, he wanted to learn, and he worked very hard to become a pitcher," Boudreau said after Lemon's passing. "He had a natural sinker and he used that to his advantage on a team that was very good defensively. He wasn't a strikeout pitcher like Feller, but he got people out. And he was a good hitter as a pitcher. He kept himself in a lot of ball games because he could hit."

Lemon retired with thirty-seven home runs, then a career record for a pitcher. To underscore baseball's amazing link, look at these two 2013 statistical bon mots: the Dodgers' Clayton Kershaw hit a home run on a opening day; the last player to do it before him was Lemon in 1953. Tim Hudson homered in the game where he won his 200th game. The last pitcher to do that? Lemon.

In 1947, he became part of an Indians' rotation that was the dominant quartet in baseball over the next decade. Lemon was the one constant from '47 to '56. The other principals in the four-man rotation were Feller (1947–54), Mike Garcia (1949–56) and Early Wynn (1949–56). Mel Harder (1947), Gene Bearden (1948–49), Art Houtteman (1954) and Herb Score (1955–56) were others who filled the fourth slot.

As great as Feller was, Lemon was the mainstay of the staff during that decade. From 1948 to 1956, he won 186 games, posting seven twenty-win seasons (1948–50, 1952–54, 1956), topped by twenty-three in 1950 and 1954. He made a minimum of thirty-one starts every season, led the league five times in complete games and a league-high ten shutouts in 1948, one of them a no-hitter.

He would have won several Cy Young Awards if the award had existed at the time. He was named pitcher of the year by the *Sporting News* three times (1948, 1950, 1954) and was the top pitcher in MVP voting those three seasons.

"Lemon would show me the curve, and it was a good curve, but he would only show it to me," Yankees legend Joe DiMaggio said in an interview with the *Press-Telegram*'s Hank Hollingworth in 1973. "He would never let me hit it. Then he would come in with the sinker that went inside and the slider that would break out. I would try to think with him, but every time I would try to think one way, Lemon would go the other."

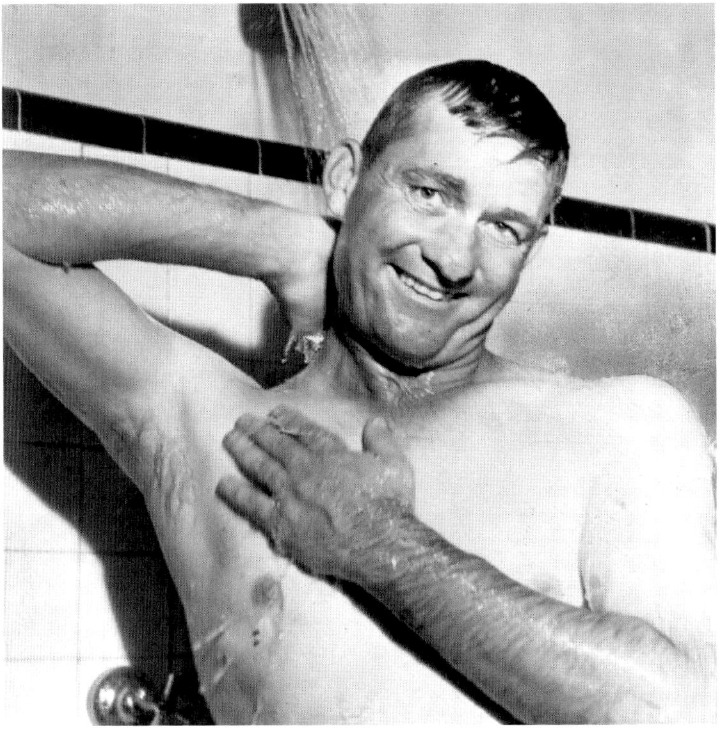

Bob Lemon takes a shower after winning his twentieth game in 1954. *Bob Keisser collection.*

The Indians won between 88 and 111 games between 1947 and 1956 and were the only team other than the Yankees to win the A.L. during that ten-year run. In 1948, the Indians won 97 games to win the American League and beat the Boston Braves in the series.

Trailing 1–0 in the series, Lemon threw a complete game and didn't allow an earned run in a 4–1 Game 2 win, a key play being his pickoff of Earl Torgeson at second to stop a Braves rally. In Game 6, with the Indians leading the series 3–2 but the series back in Boston, Lemon allowed one run in the first seven innings in a series-clinching 4–3 victory.

It was the Indians' first World Series title since 1920, back when Lemon went to the opera house with his mom.

In 1954, the Yankees won 103 games—and finished 8 games behind the Indians' record 111 wins. The '54 team would be revered for that record if they had not been swept in the series by a New York Giants team led by the magnetic Willie Mays and the Polo Grounds' unique shape.

It was Mays's catch of a drive by Vic Wertz to deepest center field at the Polo Grounds—an absurd 483 feet from home plate—with two runners on in the ninth that kept the game tied, 2–2. In the tenth, Lemon came to bat with runners on first and third with two outs and hit a shot to first base that would have scored a run if Giants manager Leo Durocher hadn't moved his first baseman off the bag before the pitch.

In the bottom of the tenth, Giants outfielder Dusty Rhodes pulled Lemon's 142nd pitch of the day down the equally absurdly short right field line—257 feet—that gave the Giants the win.

"We lost that game in the 10th when Dusty hit about a 280-foot home run into the right field bleachers off me," lamented Lemon to Doug Krikorian in the *Press-Telegram* in 1998. "If Mays doesn't make that catch, we score at least two runs and the game would have never gone into extra innings. We just never recovered from that catch." The Giants completed their sweep with an 8–4 win over Lemon, working on two days rest, in Game 4.

By 1957, time became his toughest out. He was thirty-six and no longer had the stamina that had served him so well for a decade. He was 6–12 in his last two seasons. That didn't stop the Long Beach Century Club, born in 1956, from honoring Lemon as its 1957 Athlete of the Year.

"I have been fortunate enough to have had several good years, but when you are honored after the kind of year I had in '57, it's a wonderful thing," Lemon told Jack Teele of the *Press-Telegram* on February 4, 1958.

Legendary horseman Frank Vessels, one of the charter members of the sports club that still exists today, arranged a gift for Lemon and brought "them" to the banquet: two champion heifers, who were walked on stage and made a deposit or two, plus two valuable stud assignments. They came in handy for Lemon, who had already purchased a ranch in Barstow for his parents.

Baseball wasn't done with him. He coached or worked in the front office for the Indians (1959–60), Phillies (1961) and Angels (1962–64, 1967–68) and managed in the Pacific Coast League in 1965–66 (a pennant in Seattle) and 1969. While with the Angels, Lemon would often drop off the stories of then *Press-Telegram* baseball writer Ross Newhan at the newspaper office.

In 1970, he was hired as the manager of the two-year-old Kansas City franchise and, in '71, led the Royals to an 85–76 record. He was fired by impatient management after the team struggled around .500 in 1972. Bill Veeck, who owned the Indians early in Lemon's career, hired him to manage the Chicago White Sox in 1977—a year after Lemon was voted into the Hall of Fame—and the Sox went 90–72. But Veeck sold the team, and Lemon was fired by the new owners early in 1978.

He was out of work about a week. After one of their many skirmishes with the Yankees, Steinbrenner dumped Billy Martin after a very public spat between Martin and Reggie Jackson. Steinbrenner, an Ohio native, remembered Lemon from his days as an Indians fan, plus the Yankee G.M. was former Indian third baseman Al Rosen.

The turnaround was instantaneous. Trailing by ten and a half games when he was hired, Lemon's calm replaced Martin's chaos, and the Yankees went 48–20 the rest of the way, beating the Red Sox in a one-game playoff and then the Dodgers in six games in the World Series.

"Billy taught us how to win," Yankee outfielder Lou Pinella told Loel Schrader in the October 18, 1978 *Press-Telegram*. "Lemon made it easy for us to win. He just let the players go out on the field and play. [Under Billy], there was always apprehension about what was going to happen next."

"I'm not a mental giant," Lemon said in an interview with Joe Durso of the *New York Times* on October 9, 1978. "I'm not smart enough to know whether I'm what you call a calming influence. I try to stay out of their way. These guys know how to play. I've always thought players should be left alone to rise to their own level. When I was a player, that's the way I liked it, and that's the way my managers, Lou Boudreau and Al Lopez, managed. I'm not a meddler."

Steinbrenner and Lemon remained close, which didn't mean Lemon stayed on as manager. He was let go after a 34–31 start in 1979 but rehired late in 1981 and took the Yankees to another World Series, this time losing to the Dodgers. Lemon managed just eight seasons, and only three for a full season, yet he won manager of the year three times.

Lemon remained on the Yankee payroll for several years as a scout, but he essentially spent his remaining years retired. He suffered a stroke in December 1998, two more in 1999 and passed away in January 2000.

"Bob was an inspiration to people," said Minor. "After he won two games for the Indians in the 1948 World Series, Bob was back here pumping gas at his dad's station.

"There was never a guy who was more humble. He never talked about the great things he did. If you were his friend, you were a friend for life. There were many nights Bob would call in the middle of the night and want you to come by the house. You couldn't turn him down."

"Bob was the most regular guy I've ever known in my life," said Bob Harrison, the longtime Major League baseball scout and Jordan High grad. "He never once talked about being a Hall of Famer, or about anything he did in baseball."

"I never heard Bob Lemon say an unkind word about another human being," says Stevens, the one-time St. Louis Browns and Hollywood Stars first baseman who graduated from Poly in 1937. "He might have been the nicest, kindest and most gentle man I ever met in my life."

"He was the kind of guy who liked everybody and would do anything for you," Meairs said. "I remember all of the baseball moments, but I also remember all the other times, too, when he wasn't Bob Lemon the pitcher as much as Bob Lemon, a friend."

Two years before his passing in 2000, Lemon talked about his life with the sagacity of someone at peace.

"The people I admire most are the people I grew up with," he said. "I've known them since before Wilson. They're all successful. All of them.

"It's been a wonderful life. Everything wonderful that could happen to a fellow has happened to me. Been married to the same lady for 54 years. Been living in the same house since 1949. I didn't miss much, if anything. I've seen the elephant, I've heard the owl, I've flown with the screeching eagles. No regrets."

Chapter 3

SOCKBALL

Bob Lemon's playground was Recreation Park. Tony Gwynn put in a lot of hours on Long Beach Poly's field and Blair Field, but he cut his early baseball teeth at the Gwynn Family Stadium—and not necessarily with a regulation baseball.

The Poly star and the third player from greater Long Beach to earn a spot in the Hall of Fame had more than enough moments on Major League parks to fill a memory. He hit a home run in the World Series at Yankee Stadium, got his 3,000th hit in Montreal, embraced Ted Williams at Fenway Park, accepted his Hall of Fame plaque before the largest crowd ever at Cooperstown and dropped enough hits around San Diego to own the town's heart.

But the one park and landmark the icon will always keep closest to his heart is the Gwynn Family Stadium, located in Long Beach.

It was just a narrow rectangle of a backyard on a nice, middle-class street in Long Beach, but it's where dreams of the entire Gwynn family were born. It's where a crowd of one—Tony's dad, Charles—attended every game. It's where Tony; older brother, Charles; and younger brother, Chris, played intimate family baseball games years before all three went on to play baseball in high school, college and professionally.

When Charles and Vendella Gwynn moved to Long Beach, Charles looked at the backyard and envisioned a ball field. There were trees and patio furniture there, but it was big enough for him to drop a makeshift home plate just beyond the back door and tilt it so that there was an expansive right field.

Tony Gwynn at the 1985 Long Beach Century Club awards dinner, when he was named 1984 Athlete of the Year. *From left:* his father, Charles; mother, Vendella; Tony; and his wife, Alicia.

Left field? Not so much. "How I became an opposite field hitter, I have no idea," Gwynn recalls with a huge laugh. "But if you pulled the ball, you usually lost it. Maybe that's how."

There were games nightly. When the Gwynns ran out of whiffle balls, either by losing them or hitting them so hard they cracked, they became brothers of invention. After hearing Dodgers announcer Vin Scully tell a story about the Giants' Juan Marichal making baseballs out of socks as a kid in the Dominican Republic, the Gwynns began their own production line.

Take a sock, cut it up, roll it into a lemon-sized ball and wrap it with rubber bands until it was firm. When they ran out of socks, they'd use a fig from a nearby tree as the core. When they ran out of rubber bands, they'd use whatever twine or string they could find.

There were ground rules. One of the brothers would play the role of Scully, announcing every play. Games would be played between their favorite teams—Dodgers versus Reds, for example—and each would impersonate the Major League player at bat or on the mound.

So if Tony was play-acting Joe Morgan, he'd flap his back elbow like a nervous wing. If Chris was Steve Garvey, he stood perfectly straight. If Tony was Davey

Lopes, he pulled his hair out from under his cap to impersonate Lopes's Afro. If Charles was Don Drysdale, he threw an occasional pitch high and tight.

Tony Gwynn, 3,141 major league hits later, told this story at his Hall of Fame induction ceremony. "Not one of us ever thought hitting sockballs would lead to this," he said. "Well, maybe dad."

Gwynn's career was legendary—3,141 hits, nineteenth on the all-time list and one of twenty-eight players to reach 3,000; five 200-plus hit seasons, including 220 in 1997; led the National League in batting average eight times (1984, 1987–89, 1994–97) to tie for the N.L. all-time record; fifteen All-Star games; twelve seasons receiving MVP votes; seven Silver Slugger Awards; twenty years with the same club; and a way of playing the game that embraced the youngster in all fans.

Gwynn says the real legends were his parents.

They were hardworking civil servants who wanted a rounded environment for their kids. Long Beach offered good schools, a plethora of parks and year-round youth sports programs. For tag-team parents—Charles worked days for the state, Vendella nights for the postal service—knowing there were all these positive outlets was as important as their paychecks.

"Chris and I talked about all the baseball we played as kids," Gwynn said. "We knew it would have an impact on our lives, but we just didn't know how big it would be. We talked about how we walked down to Silverado Park, playing in the streets and fields with our neighbors and friends, how we played over-the-line. How our parents would look at us in the house and say, 'Go play.'"

Charles, who passed away in 1993, saw something in his son long before Tony could understand what he was talking about. Charles Gwynn was unabashed in his support of Tony and belief that he was destined for something great.

"He saw something in me early that you can't see as a kid," Gwynn said. "He said whatever I tried to do I did well. Ping pong, baseball, whatever. He'd tell me I made things look easier. He'd come to every home [basketball] game at San Diego State and say things like that. I couldn't grasp what he was talking about.

"He just knew. He had a strange sense of knowing I was going to be pretty good, whatever it was I'd do. And we never discussed how he knew. He was a football guy, and he never once asked me to play football. He'd say 'You should do whatever you want, and I know you'll do it well.'"

But not without putting in the work. "He had a work ethic and he expected us to have one, too," Gwynn said. "He'd say, 'You have to put your dues in. Once you start, you don't quit. You follow through and finish.'

"The impact my parents had on me was monumental. There was always someone home for us. I'd come home from school, and mom would be there to talk about my day. Then my dad would come home, and he'd take us to our games. It wasn't just sports. My mom had Fridays off, so we'd all sit around and talk about the things that were important in our lives."

"Charles Gwynn was an outstanding person and father," said Joe Perruccio, a teacher and coach at Poly and one of three youth coaches Tony credits with teaching him baseball. "He was very proud of his children. He never pushed them too hard, but he told them they could succeed at anything they try."

It wasn't just Tony. Older brother Charles played several sports at Poly and was drafted in 1976 by the Cleveland Indians. He would go on to become an all-conference player at Cal State–Los Angeles and then a teacher. Younger brother Chris was also a standout at Poly, was drafted and signed by the Dodgers as a first round pick and spent ten years in the majors. He ended his career as Tony's teammate with the Padres.

"It's almost as if our dad knew our destiny, what we would achieve," said Chris. "He encouraged us all the time. And when I think back to our conversations, even those that were about baseball, they always included what we would do with our lives."

"I'm so proud of all my sons," Charles Gwynn once said. "Charles Jr. played college and is now teaching. Tony won a batting title and went to the World Series, and Chris played in the Olympic Games [1984] and now has been drafted. All that from one house in Long Beach."

As a young athlete in sports-crazy Long Beach, Tony was better known as a basketball player. In 1976, he was part of the Poly basketball team that won a CIF–Southern Section championship under head coach Ron Palmer, going 30–1 and making it look easy, winning every playoff game by eight points or more. Gwynn also was on the 1977 team that reached the title game. His gifts on the basketball court were good enough to earn him a scholarship to San Diego State.

Gwynn's best baseball exploits came in summer youth play. Poly's baseball program at the time was slumping. Whether it was park play, PONY League or American Legion, Gwynn was an impressive player. It was there that fans, scouts and coaches noticed his bat control, speed, airtight defense, work ethic and tenacious spirit.

"I was at Lakewood when they were at Poly," said local high school coaching legend John Herbold. "I remember Charles and Chris more than I do Tony. Charles had some power. Chris was very good, maybe the best high school player in the area when he played.

Tony Gwynn's younger brother, Chris, was better known than his brother as a baseball player while playing youth and high school ball (Poly) in Long Beach.

"Where I remember Tony is during the summers, when he played on legion teams and local leagues. Tony was quite a player even then. What amazed me was the way he could run. He could steal a base any time he wanted. To me, Tony is what Branch Rickey was talking about when he said, 'You don't play baseball, you work it.' Tony worked it. And he had such great focus."

Gwynn had three youth coaches in Long Beach—Joe Perruccio; his father, Isadore; and Nick Ortega. The Perruccios were all regulars at the Gwynn house, to the degree that Tony said, "They were like another set of parents."

"My dad often said Tony did things in baseball he hadn't seen since Joe DiMaggio," Joe Perruccio said. "He had the best eye-hand coordination I'd ever seen. He'd practice for three hours with our teams, then go home and play sock ball for three more. He had what I called a golden swing. There wasn't much he couldn't do with a bat."

"Nick was my Little League coach, and Mr. P and Joe were my coaches in youth leagues," Gwynn said. "They taught me the basics, the things most players hate to work on—cutoffs, relays, backing up. I think I got to the big leagues as fast as I did because of the fundamentals they taught me."

Even with that success and support, Gwynn considered leaving baseball behind to focus on basketball. He was planning to skip baseball in his senior year at Poly so he could put his mind on basketball and college. This time it was Mom who stepped up.

"She didn't think that was a good idea," he recalled. "She said, 'You might need something to fall back on.' She thought it made sense, and it did. If I hadn't played my senior year, maybe I never play baseball."

Gwynn had a scholarship offer to play basketball at Cal State-Fullerton for Bobby Dye, but when he asked then Titan baseball coach Augie Garrido if he could also play baseball, Garrido said no. He wanted full-time baseball players. Years later, Garrido joked that while he still had that philosophy, he wished he had made one exception.

Gwynn took a basketball scholarship to San Diego State and didn't even try out for the baseball team as a freshman. A friend on the basketball team, Bobby Meacham, told Aztecs coach Jim Dietz that the school's point guard was also a pretty good baseball player.

"Coach Dietz met me and said, 'Great, come on out!'" Tony said. "I sometimes wonder how different things could have been. Coach held a tryout camp each fall. If I had attended that, I would have been one of sixty guys competing, and maybe I wouldn't have been noticed."

Harry Minor, the legendary Major League scout, admits that he missed on Gwynn as a pro prospect out of high school, and he lives with the person who reminds himself of that daily.

"I remember seeing Tony as a kid and wondering if he would make it, because he wasn't strong and didn't have a great arm," Minor said. "My wife, Liz, always thought higher of Tony than I did. She was a good scout, too. Liz was working at Poly then, and she tried to talk me into it, telling me what a nice kid he was."

So why didn't he didn't heed his wife's sage advice?

"Tony could always hit," Minor said. "He could always get the bat on the ball. But he was a basketball player. He'd play basketball and come out late for baseball. And he went to San Diego State on a basketball scholarship. It just goes to show what hard work and dedication will do."

Gwynn earned all-conference honors in both basketball and baseball. The 1983 baseball and NBA drafts were held the same day, and Tony was drafted by the San Diego Padres in the third round of the baseball draft and in the tenth round of the NBA draft by the then San Diego Clippers.

"We drafted him low because everyone felt he would probably choose baseball," said Paul Silas, the Clippers coach at the time. "But we scouted him extensively. We thought he was a good shooter and defender and would make the team if we could sign him. Obviously, he made the right choice, but the skills and intelligence [he had in baseball] are a lot of the same skills he had as a basketball player."

A young Tony Gwynn at San Diego State. *Courtesy San Diego State.*

It's safe to say Gwynn made the right choice. And that work ethic never died. His fascination on improvement led him to study videotape of his at-bats nightly. He and his wife, Alicia, would take a video camera to games, tape his at-bats and review the game, home or road.

"I grinded and sucked up every bit of information I could get," Gwynn said. "Using video was just something that worked for me, because the more information I had, the better I would perform." He laughingly adds that he's the only man who has all of his hits on videotape.

Gwynn had a career .392 on-base percentage and struck out only 434 times in 9,288 at-bats. He had a career slugging percentage of .459, better than similar contemporaries like Wade Boggs, Lou Brock, Rod Carew and Pete Rose, and he drove in more runs (1,138) than anyone in that group, with the exception of Rose.

He stole 319 bases, hit .306 in the postseason and .371 in his two World Series appearances and came as close as anyone to breaking the .400 standard in more than a half-century. He was hitting .394 in 1994 when baseball went on strike and didn't come back. One will always wonder if he could have been the first to hit .400 in the National League since Bill Terry in 1930 or the first in the majors since Ted Williams did it in 1941.

He ended his career with an average of .338, which ranks eighteenth all time and the highest ranked modern-era player. Ted Williams, whose last season was 1961, is the most contemporary player ranked higher.

He won eight National League batting titles, sharing the record with Honus Wagner and only Ty Cobb (twelve) had more in baseball history. He holds the National League record for consecutive seasons hitting .300 at nineteen, and only Cobb (twenty-four) had a longer streak.

"I gravitated to those kind of hitters, Rose, Brett, Boggs, guys who would rack up two or three hits a game," Gwynn said. "I never had much success trying to hit balls out of the park and be that kind of run producer, and I didn't even think about it until I had my first chance to talk to Ted Williams about it."

When the two first met, they talked baseball for hours, and they became very close friends. At the 1999 All-Star game at Fenway Park, Williams was driven to the pitcher's mound in a golf cart as part of the pre-game pageantry, and Gwynn was the first to greet him and help him out of the cart. Williams was mobbed by the All-Stars, who gathered around him like a baseball mosh pit.

Williams advised Gwynn to stop thinking of singles. "When we met, he picked up my bat, frowned, then put it up to his mouth and said, 'I can pick my teeth with this,'" Gwynn said.

"I always thought [home runs] were boring. I felt I had to work at my craft and understand what I did best and what I needed to do to get better. And that was make contact. I thrived on situations where a single would score the winning run," he said. Gwynn had a career average of .458 with the bases loaded. "That's sort of a lost art now."

A rather trim Tony Gwynn waits his turn at the batting cage in his early years with the San Diego Padres. *Bob Keisser collection.*

Gwynn listened, and he wound up posting some of his best power numbers. Of Gwynn's 135 career home runs, 43 came in his last three full seasons (1997–99), after he had chatted with Williams, including a career high 17 in 1997, a year in which he also posted his most hits in a season (220), his most RBIs (110) and his highest average (.372) in a full season.

Ted said something to Gwynn once that resonated on the day he was inducted. "He said, 'When you retire, you'll know whether you've done a good job by the people that come out.'" The day Gwynn and Cal Ripken Jr. were inducted, 75,000 people attended, the largest crowd in the history of the Hall of Fame ceremony. Fans filled the long grass field from the stage to an endless horizon. It was baseball's version of Woodstock.

Gwynn, now the baseball coach at his alma mater, San Diego State, and recovering from surgery for throat cancer, mentioned Ted in his Hall of Fame speech, but he saved his finest words for his dad.

"This would have been an event he would have loved to be at," he said. "He always said work hard and good things will happen, and boy, was he right.

"I learned from him that you had to do extra, and I did do the extra things necessary to get here. But really, that's all we really ask of each other. We make a big deal about having a good work ethic, but that's what we're supposed to have."

Chapter 4

THE DUKE OF COMPTON

Long before the entire population of Brooklyn and greater New York knew him as the Duke of Flatbush, he was the Duke of Compton.

Duke Snider owned a piece of Brooklyn's heart for the eleven years he played at Ebbets Field, the biggest chunk of his seventeen-year Major League career. He hit 175 of his 407 career home runs at Ebbets, most of them over the Schaefer Beer sign atop the right field scoreboard and bounding down Bedford Avenue with a passel of young Dodgers fans giving chase.

His father, Wade, gave Edwin Donald Snider the nickname "Duke" because his young son had a regal walk, and Duke was without question the player who exuded royalty in the Dodgers' royal blue colors. He hit 407 career home runs, which was tenth on the all-time list when he retired in 1964; hit .298; and was inducted into the Baseball Hall of Fame in 1980.

He was part of the one of the greatest dynasties in baseball, in terms of fan fervor and affection, if not wins. The Dodgers from 1947 to 1962 went to the World Series eight times; won twice, once on each coast; and lost two heartbreaking playoff series to their rival Giants, again, one on each coast.

The Dodgers won 1,545 games in those sixteen seasons (96.5 per), and there are more than a dozen members of the Hall of Fame connected to those teams, including an owner (Walter O'Malley), general manager (Branch Rickey), manager (Walt Alston) and enough players to fill out a lineup card.

But for all of his ties to Brooklyn, Snider had less-known, subtle roles in several areas of Southern California baseball—as one of the finest talents to

A rare picture of Duke Snider when he was at Compton High, which was the campus for both the two-year high school and junior college. Snider played quarterback/halfback.

emerge from greater Long Beach to the Major League, as a contemporary of Jackie Robinson as he broke baseball's color barrier and as a bridge to baseball's expansion to the West Coast.

Snider grew up in Lynwood, went to school in Compton and played baseball wherever he could, including a lot of parks in Long Beach, like the seminal Recreation Park, built in 1924. When the Dodgers contacted him for a tryout in 1943, it was held at Rec Park.

Snider went to Compton's Washington Elementary School and Enterprise Junior High, which served grades seven to ten in the '40s. By the time he was in his teens, he already had won notices on youth and semipro baseball teams, including the Compton Merchants, where he often played with and against ballplayers five to ten years older.

His coaches back then were Chet Crain, who coached at Compton College and was a city council member; Ramon Gonzalez, who ran a sporting goods store and eventually became president of the school district; Joe Rozelle, the uncle of one of his best friends in high school, a lad named Pete Rozelle, who went on to mold the NFL as its commissioner; and his high school coach, Bill Schleibaum.

"We played all over, most often at Compton Crestview Park, which became Gonzalez Park, named after Ramon, who was Mr. Baseball in Compton," Snider said. "He was like a father to me when my dad went into the navy in World War II.

"I played on the same semipro team out of Montebello as Gene Mauch (the Major League manager) and in youth leagues in Compton and Long Beach. Even during the off-season, I'd play double-headers on Sundays in the fall and winter at parks all over. There were always games at Rec Park."

Snider was a three-sport star at Compton High, which served kids in grades eleven and twelve and also was the campus for Compton College, and earned all-league honors in all three. He led the basketball team in scoring as a senior playing alongside Rozelle.

Compton met Long Beach Poly for the league title that season at the old Long Beach Auditorium. "Pete had a good set shot from the baseline and Poly had these big six-footers, so we decided to feed him the ball," Snider recalled with a smile. "Well, Pete missed his first six shots and we didn't give him the ball any more."

In football, Snider played halfback in a single-wing attack and led Compton to a league title. He earned second-team All-CIF honors behind Glenn Davis, who was CIF Player of the Year at Bonita High and later won the Heisman Trophy at Army. In the Compton-Poly game that year, Compton trailed by six points with less than two minutes to go when Snider threw a sixty-five-yard touchdown pass for the tie and completed a conversion toss for the win.

"Pete often said that if the timing had been right, I could have made a good pro quarterback," Snider said. "He was impressed with the way I threw the ball so accurately."

Rozelle was good at helping people's images. He wrote for the school newspaper and also was a stringer for the *Long Beach Press-Telegram*, getting Duke several headlines in the process. The tie was so strong that the *Press-Telegram*'s headline on Rozelle's being named NFL president was, "Snider Press Agent named NFL Chief."

"He was all bony arms and legs, a whirlwind," his high school coach Schleibaum said in the August 1956 issue of *Sport Magazine*. "Nobody could name his best sport. He wanted to play outfield, but he had such an arm that he won eight straight games for me pitching. In football, I played him at defensive end and tailback. In basketball, he was all over the floor."

In the wake of the joyous 1955 World Series, Duke Snider sits in front of his Ebbets Field locker with several bats and his number 4 uniform hanging in the background. *Bob Keisser collection.*

Snider earned All-CIF honors in the lone season of high school ball as a junior, hitting .411. He pitched when he wasn't playing center field and threw a no-hitter in a tournament at Beverly Hills High School. He didn't play as a senior; he signed with the Brooklyn Dodgers in January 1944 so he could get some pro experience before going into the military.

"My dad was in the service and I knew I would be drafted later that year when I turned 18," Snider said. "I had these offers to go to college and they were attractive, but I'd still be going into the service. Baseball was my best sport and I could graduate in February, so it made sense for me to sign a contract and get a year of professional experience in before going to the war."

He played in 133 minor league games in 1944 before spending all of 1945 and half of 1946 in the service. He spent part of it in Guam and the balance in a Long Beach naval post. He split 1947 and 1948 between Brooklyn and the minors and then became a regular in 1949, hitting 307 home runs in the next nine seasons, including 40 or more in five straight seasons (1953–57), a feat neither Mickey Mantle nor Willie Mays ever accomplished.

The April, 1956 edition of *Sports Illustrated* gave Snider a superb scouting report: "Physically, he was the perfect ballplayer—tremendous left-handed power, vast fielding skill, a fine arm."

"[Duke] was an extremely gifted talent and his defensive abilities were often overlooked because of playing in a small ballpark [Ebbets]," Dodgers legendary announcer Vin Scully said after Snider's passing. "When he had a chance to run and move defensively, he had the grace and the abilities of DiMaggio and Mays."

Snider brought something else to Brooklyn: a contemporary view of race relations. He grew up watching Robinson star at Muir High, Pasadena City College and UCLA and quickly began to idolize his gifts.

"I saw Jackie when I was in junior high," Snider wrote in his autobiography. "[I] saw him play a baseball game, leave in the middle of it and trot over to compete in the broad jump in a track meet, and then run back and finish the baseball game."

The fact that Robinson was African American never wrinkled Snider's view. Southern California's diversity was a given for Snider. Many of Snider's coaches and closest friends were Hispanic. Snider saw many Asian teammates on his semipro teams disappear during internment. Race held no distinction for someone who loved playing ball and respected anyone who did likewise.

"He wanted to tell me how, back in Los Angeles, he had seen Jackie excel at football, baseball, basketball and track," former Dodger teammate Ralph Branca said, to the *New York Times*, after Snider's passing. "He trumpeted Jackie's athleticism and was thrilled at the prospect of playing with him."

"(Robinson) was the greatest competitor I've ever seen," Snider said. "I've seen him beat a team with his bat, his ball, his glove, his feet and, in a game in Chicago one time, with his mouth. He'd put on his game face and was all business. He showed his intensity by his example on the field."

"Jackie knew he had to do well," Snider said in his Hall of Fame induction speech. "He knew that the future of blacks in baseball depended on it. The pressure was enormous, overwhelming and unbearable at times. I don't know how he held up. I know I never could have."

The Dodgers' move to Los Angeles was one of the worst things to ever happen to Brooklyn, and Snider knew that. "It was great to be returning home when the team moved to Los Angeles, but there was no doubt that we were leaving something special behind in Brooklyn," he said.

But it was a boon to baseball's rise to a true national pastime. Snider and Don Drysdale were pivotal parts of the move West since they were natives of the area. Drysdale played baseball at Van Nuys High. They were the first ambassadors of Dodger baseball in Los Angeles. Many of the promotional efforts to spread the word of Dodger baseball were fronted by Snider and Drysdale.

The move wasn't a boon for Snider's career. Ebbets was an intimate bandbox for a left-handed slugger. The Dodgers' first home in Los Angeles was the Grand Canyon in comparison.

The L.A. Coliseum was built for the 1932 Olympics and served well as a football stadium. As a baseball park, it was a freak. The left-field screen was ridiculously close at 251 feet, and the club compensated by making right field look like the sixteenth fairway at Augusta. Dead center field was 425 feet away, and a fence then fanned out a preposterous 440 feet to the right field gap. It then straightened out to 390 feet across the field running parallel to Figueroa Street before a steep turn the last 10 feet or so at the foul pole.

Snider's home runs fell from forty in 1957 to fifteen in 1958. He hit just six home runs at the Coliseum that season, and not a single one was to right field, which has to be one of the most extreme statistical oddities in baseball history. The fences were modestly moved in some in 1959, and Snider hit twenty-three home runs, fifteen at the Coliseum.

Snider already had 316 career home runs after the 1957 season at the age of thirty-one. Using a formula popularized by sabermetrics guru Bill James, which projects the number of years a player has left and his most recent stats, Snider began 1957 with a 50 percent chance of reaching 500 home runs.

He finished his career with 407. The four seasons playing in the Coliseum pasture (1958–61) cost him severely.

"We didn't play any games at the Coliseum before arriving from spring training," Snider said. "We had heard all the stories about the short fence in left, but we didn't hear much about right field except that it was big.

"Before that first game [against the Giants, who left New York with the Dodgers], we were part of a downtown parade, so we got to the Coliseum late, after the Giants. Willie Mays comes out of his locker room to find me, and he's laughing so hard, and he says, 'Duke, I've got to show you something.' So we walk to the field, and Mays points to right field and said 'Duke, they just buried you.'"

Snider didn't lament the lost stats. "The Coliseum did take some away," he said. "I hit a lot of 400-foot outs. But I can't look at it that way. I lost a lot more to my knee injuries."

Snider had knee surgery in the off-season before 1958, reinjured it in a car accident during spring training and couldn't turn on his repaired knee until June. He also strained his right elbow trying to throw a ball out of the Coliseum, which earned him a fine, and was beaned by a foul ball while leading off third. The knee injuries lingered, and he only had more than three hundred at-bats three times in his last seven seasons.

"If I had stayed healthy and been able to play every day until I was thirty-seven instead of sporadically as I did, I might have reached those numbers. But in 1958, I was probably 70 percent of the player I was in 1957."

The 1959 season was much better. It was the last hurrah for the Boys of Summer—Snider, Gil Hodges, Johnny Podres, Carl Erskine, Carl Furillo and Pee Wee Reese (as a coach). The remnants of the '55 World Champs teamed with a nucleus of young players to win the 1959 World Series.

"We knew we weren't the same players we were in Brooklyn," Snider said. "We were really a deteriorating club in 1958. We won in 1959 because the old guys wanted to show they could still play, and we had a lot of new guys who benefited from our experience."

Snider's last season with the Dodgers was 1962, when he hit .278 with a .418 on-base percentage on a team that won 102 games but lost a 3-game playoff to the Giants. He took a victory lap with the Mets near Brooklyn in 1963 before an incongruous ending in 1964 with the Giants.

Snider passed away in 2011. For many Dodgers fans, the last memories came from 2008, when the Dodgers celebrated their fiftieth anniversary in Los Angeles by first playing an exhibition at the Coliseum against the Red Sox. A crowd of 115,300 crammed the hastily reconfigured park, which this time had a left-field fence even closer than the original from 1958.

Two days later, the Dodgers opened the season at Dodger Stadium with fans expecting the introduction of former players. What they got instead was a slow procession of the past, beginning when the gate in center field opened and Duke Snider walked slowly to his former position to a cacophony of cheers—no announcers, no over-the-top presentation. Just a slow, volcanic rumination on history beginning with the most royal of all the Dodgers: the Duke of Flatbush, the young man who welcomed Jackie Robinson to the Major Leagues, the bridge to so many memories that began in Compton.

Chapter 5

MONEYBALL, PART I

True Grich

The only thing harder than gaining entrance to baseball's Hall of Fame is breaking into Fort Knox, and a lot of great baseball players would sooner grab a shovel and dig for gold than wait for that elusive call from Cooperstown.

Wilson's Bob Lemon was the dominant American League pitcher for a decade, but it took him twelve voting cycles before the Baseball Writers Association of America (BBWAA) voted him into the Hall. Compton's Duke Snider, part of the Mays-Mantle-Snider New York trilogy of greats, had to wait eleven years to be elected.

Wilson standout Grich, on the other hand, stayed on the Hall of Fame ballot for only one year, just like Tony Gwynn. The former Orioles and Angels second baseman did so, though, only because he didn't get enough votes to stay on the ballot a second year.

Grich thus has become the reigning subject of the Society for American Baseball Research (SABR) crowd about Hall of Fame worthiness. As far as the men who crunch numbers for a living and the sheer fun of baseball are concerned, Grich's situation is as much of a crime as stealing America's gold.

When he hit the ballot in 1992, he received just eleven votes. Grich's 2.6 percentage of the vote—5.0 was required—knocked him off the ballot. Hindsight isn't just twenty-twenty when it comes to Grich; it has the power of the Hubble telescope. Bobby Grich should be in the Hall. By all the new standards made popular through sabermetrics and a lot of the old ones, Grich should have a plaque in Cooperstown.

Former Wilson star Bobby Grich takes batting practice in 1984 before an Angels home game.

In his seventeen seasons with the Orioles and Angels, he had a .984 career fielding percentage and hit 224 home runs. In Major League history, only six second basemen have hit more: Jeff Kent (377), Rogers Hornsby (301), Craig Biggio (291), Ryne Sandberg (288), Joe Morgan (268) and Joe Gordon (253). That's four Hall of Famers and two players who should be elected in the next few years.

His career "secondary average" of .330, which is essentially all of the major hitting stats, ranks him eighth all time. He had a longer career than half of the aforementioned six and had the best defensive stats of almost everyone else.

The writers who covered his career in Baltimore and Los Angeles knew he was special, and so did his teammates. He just never caught on with the national media.

As *L.A. Times* columnist Jim Murray wrote on September 4, 1986, "An imposing physical specimen for a second baseman—or for a right fielder, for all of that—Grich looks like a lumber yard to an opposing pitcher. But he seldom overpowers a pitch on sheer strength. He rarely tries to. Bobby renders to pitchers the things that are pitchers."

Using Bill James's Wins Above Replacement stat, Grich ranks fifty-ninth on the all-time list, all players at all positions, with Hornsby, Eddie Collins, Nap Lajoie and Joe Morgan as the only second basemen ranked higher. James ranked Grich twelfth on his all-time list of second baseman in his seminal 1988 book, *The Historical Baseball Abstract*, ahead of eight Hall of Famers.

"No player in history is truly comparable to Grich," wrote James, "which in itself is evidence of his quality. He was a hidden star who created a lot of runs for someone with a .260–.270 average."

Grich ranks eleventh all-time in double plays for a second baseman; ninth all-time in zone runs, which is a nouveau gauge of how many ground balls he reaches;

Former Bruin Grich was one of the best defensive second basemen of his era.

and fifth in range factor per nine innings (5.687). The closest Hall of Famer to Grich on that list is Sandberg at twenty-eighth.

Rich Lederer is Long Beach's resident baseball analyst and publisher of the *Baseball Analysts* website that attracts most of the baseball literati for its advanced perspective and knowledgeable opinions. Lederer is also a second-generation Long Beach institution; his dad, George, was the first Dodgers beat writer at the *Press-Telegram* and later worked for the Angels.

Lederer made his HOF case for Grich in 2008 when Joe Gordon was elected by the veteran's committee. "Gordon's induction should open up the doors to Cooperstown for Grich. Not to take anything away from Gordon but Grich was every bit as good as the Hall's newest member, both defensively and offensively," Lederer wrote.

Lederer noted that Gordon's career slash line was .268/.357/.466 with a OPS+ (on-base plus slugging, adjusted for era and parks) of 120. Grich had Gordon in OBP (.371) and OPS+ (125). Grich's career numbers came at a time when the league average for a second baseman was 259/.324/.384.

"Grich and Gordon were two of the best second basemen in the game's history," Lederer said. "Gordon posted a .970 (career) fielding percentage, leading the AL in assists four times and double plays three times. Grich had a .983 fielding percentage while leading the AL in assists, putouts, and double plays for three straight seasons. He committed only five errors and set a then major-league record with a .995 fielding percentage in 1973 when all 12 American League fields were grass."

Lederer also used a newer stat too—Win Shares—to further make his case. "[Win Shares] is as reliable as any other when combining offense and defense to compare two players such as Gordon and Grich," he said.

Gordon had 242 career win shares and a 21.07 average per 162 games; Grich had 329 career win shares and a 26.54 rank. "[Grich] had 36 percent more career Win Shares with better peak seasons and a much higher rate per 162 games. Whether your preference is quantity or quality, Grich gets the nod here," Lederer said.

Gordon had some advantages. He won the A.L. MVP award in 1942, even though Ted Williams won the Triple Crown that same season. He also played on five World Series champion teams and was a star on the beloved Yankees. Grich never got into the World Series.

The 1992 ballot was also one of the most vexing ever. It included one automatic, Tom Seaver, who was voted in on his first try and received the highest number of votes in Hall of Fame history. It also included Rollie Fingers, who made it on his second try to become only the second closer to make the Hall.

Orlando Cepeda was on the ballot for the thirteenth time, his candidacy complicated by a marijuana arrest. Former Pirates star Bill Mazeroski, long considered the greatest fielding second baseman ever, was making his fifteenth and last appearance on the ballot; he'd eventually make the Hall via the veteran's committee. Fan favorite and Cubs third baseman Ron Santo was on the ballot for the ninth time. (He also made it, much too late, via the vets).

The polarizing Dick Allen was also a candidate, and there were forty-one write-in votes for the banned Pete Rose. With all of those candidates, maybe Grich just got lost in the maze.

The man himself harbors no grudge, and he understands how his defensive work might have been overlooked at the time.

"I was disappointed and surprised," he said. "But as I started to work for the Angels front office, I'd come out to the games and spend time in the press box and started to watch the game from the writer's perspective.

"The game flows, and someone hits a two-run home run that puts his team ahead. As the game goes on, maybe it's the seventh inning and the bases are loaded with two outs and someone hits a sinking line drive and the left fielder makes a great catch. And the next day, the story is Frank Robinson or Boog Powell hit a two-run home run to win the game, and the shoestring catch by Paul Blair gets lost in the story.

"As a player, I know what a play like Blair's means. It's a deciding factor, without a shadow of a doubt. But for the story-tellers (media), it's not the big headline. I'll be honest, too. I knew how important defense was to the game, but not in the detail of runs allowed and runs stopped that we do today."

Grich always thought he had good range for a second baseman, and then someone put it into run context. In 1973, Grich's hitting line was .251/.373/.387, and he led the A.L. in defensive chances (945) while making just five errors. His Wins Above Replacement (WAR) total was 4.7 for offense and 3.9 for defense. His defense saved twenty-nine runs above average.

Minnesota's Rod Carew had a hitting line of .350/.411/.471. His hitting WAR was 6.7, but his defensive WAR was -0.5. Defensively, he saved -0.5 runs. One can argue to death the value of offense to defense, but the stats clearly show that Grich's hitting and defense that year netted more runs for the Orioles than Carew did the Twins.

"It puts a number on the kind of things you learn that's part of baseball but has rarely been [quantified]," Grich said, though he wasn't talking about the Carew example. "It's knowing the hitter, cheating on a pitch sometimes by ten feet because I know a slow curve is probably headed to second base. There were days when I'd play ten feet further in because of the field condition."

"I have no hard feelings. I never did anything on a national platform, in the All-Star game or the playoffs, never had that shiny moment. I had some good hitting years but never played in a park like Fenway or Wrigley where I might have hit fifty more home runs. I lost a few years to injuries. The disc injury in 1977 cost me a whole year and hurt me for two, and I broke my hand twice. It's just nice that people are talking about this now."

Given some time and a push from Lederer and other baseball writers, maybe Grich will get his day in the Hall.

He's certainly in the Long Beach Hall. Grich was a two-sport star at Wilson, as a shortstop who hit .365 his senior season in baseball and a quarterback in football who led the Bruins to a 9–2 record in 1965 with sixteen touchdown passes and five rushing. UCLA offered him a football scholarship, and some scouts felt the solidly built six foot two Grich had professional potential. Tommy Prothro was the Bruins coach at the time, and he had Grich penciled in as the heir to Gary Beban.

"I loved him as a baseball player," said resident Long Beach baseball scout Harry Minor. "There were football scouts and coaches out there who thought Grich had the potential to win the Heisman Trophy. Skip Rowland [the former Wilson baseball coach] loved him. Once Skip started talking about Bobby, you couldn't shut him up.

"I took a second look at him because of Skip and recommended him to our cross-checker [when Minor was a Mets scout]. I knew the Baltimore scout who was following Bob and he said he was the kind of ballplayer who would do whatever it took to win games. That's the kind of things some people overlook."

When the Orioles drafted him with the nineteenth pick in the first round of the amateur draft, things got complicated. "I already had my fall schedule, was rushing a fraternity and had a dorm room when I was drafted," Grich said. "The Orioles offered $25,000, and my dad said no. Then they said $30,000, and my dad said no."

The give-and-take ended when the Orioles offered $42,500 and his dad said OK—as long as the team would let him play baseball just in the summer so he could attend college. He spent his first summer playing rookie ball in Bluefield and then his second for Stockton in the California League. "I'd fly up for weekend games while school was still in session," Grich said.

He was two quarters into his sophomore year when the Orioles invited him to the Major League spring training camp. "My dad said a year and two quarters was enough, but he always wanted me to finish school," Grich said. Which he did, continuing his education at Fresno State and Long Beach State during off-seasons. "I always felt I wanted a degree so I could coach if things didn't work out."

That first full-time season was difficult. He hit .227 in Stockton. But he learned to stop pulling the ball while there, and his career took off. He spent 1970 in Texas League AA ball and split 1971 in Texas and the O's AAA team in Rochester. In 1971, he was named Minor League Baseball's MVP with a massive line of stats in Rochester—.336 average, .439 on-base, .632 slugging, thirty-two home runs and eighty-three RBIs.

He received call-ups to the Orioles in 1970 (30 games) and 1971 (7) before he finally landed in Baltimore for good. But he still had to fight for playing time because Mark Belanger and Davey Johnson were incumbents at short and second. Despite that, he got into 133 games and hit .278 with twelve home runs.

Once Grich became a regular in 1973, he stayed there for the rest of his career with the Orioles (1970–76) and Angels (1977–86). He missed part of the '77 season because of a back problem but otherwise was an everyday player until his last two seasons. He had double-digit home runs in twelve seasons, with a high of thirty (with 101 RBIs) in 1979 and twenty-two to lead in the American League in the strike-shortened 1981 season.

He ended his career with 1,833 hits, 1,097 walks, 1,033 runs scored, 320 doubles, 224 home runs, an on-base percentage of .371 and slugging of

.424. He led the A.L. in putouts four times and assists and range factor three times while winning four Gold Glove awards.

He continues to work for the Angels in community and alumni relations, proving that some players never lose their range.

Chapter 6

MONEYBALL, PART II

The Shutout of Vern Stephens

Bobby Grich had it good, Hall of Fame–wise, compared to Vern Stephens.

Before Bob Lemon made it to the pitching rotation of the Cleveland Indians, Vern Stephens had already arrived as the best Major League player out of Long Beach. The Poly and Long Beach City College product was part of the late-'30s entourage of local ballplayers who reached the Major Leagues in 1941, and by 1942, he was the star player of the St. Louis Browns.

Between 1942 and 1950, he made the American League All-Star team seven times. He finished in the top ten in MVP balloting six times, including third in 1944, tops among hitters, when he led the A.L. in RBIs with 109 and was second in home runs (twenty), and fourth in 1942 and 1948. He led the A.L. in RBIs two other times, 1949 and 1950, when he had 159 and 144, respectively, while hitting behind Ted Williams in the Boston Red Sox lineup. He had more walks than strikeouts in his career.

He led the league in assists by a shortstop three times (1947–49) and was second twice (1944–45). He finished in the top four in double plays five times. His range factor—like Grich, two words never mentioned when the two men played—was always among the highest in the league.

In a statistical ranking of players, he is considered the 203rd best in the 150-plus years of the game, and his Wins Above Replacement (WAR) ranking is 41.8, which is the 237th best. He outranks numerous shortstops who are in the Hall of Fame, including Dave Bancroft, Rabbit Maranville, Joe Tinker and Phil Rizzuto.

A young Vern Stephens during his early days with the St. Louis Browns. Stephens was the best player on the only Browns team to win a pennant, in 1944. *Bob Keisser Collection.*

In 1942, he led the Browns to their best record in two decades, and he was doing it with an inferior product. During the war, baseball was using a cheaper baseball, called the balata ball, which often died on impact. In 1944, he led the Browns to their only World Series. And when the Browns ran into financial problems after the 1947 season, they traded Stephens to the Red Sox for six players and $310,000.

When he retired after the 1955 season, he had 247 career home runs, 213 of them as a shortstop—the most of any shortstop in baseball history at that time.

The year he was first eligible for the Hall of Fame was 1962. And he didn't get a single vote.

"I think he's one of the most underrated and undervalued players in history," longtime scout Harry Minor said. "He was a power hitter who played shortstop and had a helluva arm. He was the best player on his team [the Browns], and Ted Williams had some great seasons because Stephens was hitting behind him. He started two All-Star games and was the cleanup hitter. How do you overlook someone like that?"

Nowadays, the men who crunch stats for a living look at Stephens's numbers and can only assume that the voters in 1962 found a variety of ways to diminish Stephens's accomplishments.

Bill James, the guru of new statistics, doesn't equivocally say that Stephens is a Hall of Famer. But in his 1994 book *The Politics of Glory*, he makes it clear that Stephens was severely underrated. He wrote that Stephens and Stan Musial broke into baseball the same year (1941) and that Stephens had superior power numbers for the first decade of their careers.

"Granted, Musial's other statistics...were better, but Stephens was a shortstop...who was driving in far more runs," James wrote. He noted the two were playing on the same home field, too, Sportsman's Park, which favored left-handed hitters, not right-handers like Stephens.

James's chapter compares the careers of Stephens and Yankees icon Phil Rizzuto, detailing the love affair the media had with the Yankees and how it impacted award voting and the Hall of Fame.

In 1949, Stephens had thirty-nine home runs, 159 RBIs, hit .290 and additionally led the league in assists by a shortstop—"one of the greatest years with the bat that any shortstop had ever had," wrote James—and he finished seventh in MVP voting. Rizzuto had an average of .275, walked 72 times to Stephen's 101, scored three fewer runs and had five home runs and 65 RBIs, and he finished second.

Writers had easy excuses. The Browns were perennial losers who were runners-up in their own city to the Cardinals, and the Western edge of Major League Baseball suffered in terms of coverage. His first five seasons came during World War II, and numbers from that era are widely discounted since many "real players" were serving in the military. Stephens suffered a knee injury as a kid, and every time he was examined by army doctors, they classified him 4F, unfit for service.

In 1946, he was one of a handful of stars who briefly jumped for a big payday in the Mexican League and then were scoffed at by the media when they came home.

When he put up massive numbers from 1948 to 1951 with the Red Sox, he was hitting behind Ted Williams and playing in Fenway with the Green Monster in left field. The Red Sox never got to the World Series, either, losing a one-game playoff in 1948—to Lemon and the Cleveland Indians—and losing the 1949 A.L. title on the last day of the season.

His career took a nosedive starting in 1951, when he was bothered by back problems. He played out the last five years as a damaged veteran with a reputation for living the high life, sharing drinks in clubs with comely ladies. "He was a good-looking bastard and the women loved him, and he tried to accommodate them all," said his former Browns teammate Ellis Clary.

By the time he was eligible for the Hall of Fame ballot in 1962, the St. Louis Browns had been gone for eight years, having moved to Baltimore in 1954. He was twelve years removed from his last great season, and the Hall of Fame ballot was stuffed with future Hall of Famers. There were an astounding thirty-seven players on the 1962 ballot who eventually made it into the Hall.

Vern Stephens (right) checks out the seating arrangement with fellow Long Beach icons Chuck Stevens (left) and Ron Fairly (center) at the 1965 Long Beach Century Club banquet.

In 2008, the Hall of Fame shook up its Veterans Committee policy, and Stephens returned to a ballot. One player was elected: former Yankee Joe Gordon, a second baseman whose numbers are comparable to Stephens and who provided a similar counterpoint to Bobby Grich in the previous chapter.

"Stephens's case is certainly more interesting than the 2008 committee thought it was," said Rich Lederer, the creator of the popular *Baseball Analysts* website and son of former *Long Beach Press-Telegram* George Lederer. "They gave him less than 25 percent of the vote, while Gordon got 83 percent.

"He's clearly among the best-hitting shortstops of all time, with a career that was just a bit too short to compile overwhelming counting stats, and he was at the very least a pretty decent fielding shortstop. That's difficult to assess, but five shortstops with similar careers are in the Hall of Fame."

Stephens was born on the road. The family was moving west to Long Beach when he arrived prematurely while driving through New Mexico. He was a bit of a runt as a kid (five foot five, 120 pounds) but was already good enough to play in the same American Legion crowd as Lemon and to be a second-team All-CIF pick in 1937. His breakout came a year later at Long Beach City College when his body filled out. He hit .552 at LBCC and signed in 1938 with the Browns for $500.

"You can imagine how an 18-year-old kid, whose dad was a milkman, went for that," Stephens said in 1948. "That early-to-bed and early-to-rise routine had failed to make my dad wealthy, despite the proverb. Of course, $500 isn't much as bonuses go now. [But] it was unusual then, when boys were begging for a chance to get into professional baseball," he said in the August 11, 1948 issue of *The Sporting News.*

Stephens's desire probably cost him a few dollars. Boston Red Sox scout Earl Sheely came by his home a few days after he signed with the Browns and was prepared to pay a lot more than $500.

He was in the majors by 1941. A teammate that season was his Poly and American Legion teammate, first baseman Chuck Stevens.

"The guy's stats were astounding," Stevens said of Stephens. "He had a great baseball mind, and he could do it all as a player. He could run, field and hit, and he also had a good arm.

"We were roommates together in the minor leagues and came up together with the Browns in '41," Stevens told Krikorian in a September 2005 *Press-Telegram* interview. "I'll never forget that year being at Yankee Stadium for the first time, two kids from Long Beach in awe of playing in the same place where Ruth and Gehrig had played and where DiMaggio still was playing. It was a memorable experience."

The Red Sox finally got Stephens in 1948, where he played alongside Hall of Famers Williams, second baseman Bobby Doerr, Joe DiMaggio's brother Dom and beloved Red Sox infielder Johnny Pesky.

He started the season slowly. "I guess I was pressing a little too hard," he said. "I knew the Red Sox had bought me to bring Boston a pennant. I was tightened up, perhaps unconsciously.

"(Red Sox manager) Joe McCarthy straightened me out. He simply told me to play the way I had for the Browns and he'd be perfectly satisfied. Just be yourself," Stephens said in the Sporting News article.

Stephens, who still holds a Major League record for most hits in an inning (three, shared with Johnny Damon and three nineteenth-century players), was very well liked during his career, mostly because of a friendly demeanor, a lot of personality and a great work ethic.

He never complained about playing for the Browns, a woebegone team with no following. In the 1944 pennant season, the Browns averaged 6,606

Bill Veeck (center) was the owner of the St. Louis Browns when Vern Stephens (left) played for them and the owner of the Cleveland Indians briefly when Bob Lemon (right) was the ace starter.

fans a game. He never complained when he was moved to third base later in his career.

"I can never recall an instance when Stephens wasn't hustling," his Browns manager, Muddy Ruel, said in 1947 and noted in the 1948 *TSN* article. "What made me appreciate him was the fact that during the first month of the season he was hitting about .220. You know with a last-place club there's always an inclination to drift to the same level when there isn't much incentive. But with Stephens it was a matter of pride. He was out there hustling.

"He was an awfully strong guy who could hit a ball a long ways," said his Red Sox teammate Johnny Pesky. "He also was very fast, and a sure fielder. He filled a need for us, and batted cleanup behind Ted Williams. He was a very unpretentious guy, and there was nothing conceited about him at all. He was a great guy to be around."

"He was one of the nicest people you'd ever want to meet, and everyone who knew him liked him," his former teammate Stevens said. "I never, ever, heard anyone utter a cross word about him."

"I think what hurt Vern about the Hall of Fame was that he didn't have enough longevity," Eddie Bockman, the 1938 Wilson High graduate and contemporary of Stephens who played in the majors and served as a scout for decades, told Krikorian in 2005. "He had three great years in Boston, and six in St. Louis.

"I remember playing against him when I was at Wilson and he was at Poly. What a hitter! We'd handle him like they handled Barry Bonds. He was such a good person, and it's a shame his life was cut so short. He got cheated."

Stephens died young, at forty-eight in 1968. He was working two good jobs, public relations for a trucking company and as a manager for Hillerich-Bradsby, the maker of Louisville Slugger bats, and was a scratch golfer who many said could have competed on the PGA tour.

He was one of the best amateurs in California for many years after leaving baseball and played in many Pro-Ams, including the Bing Crosby National at Pebble Beach. He shot a seventy-five at Meadowlark Golf Course one day and died of a heart attack the next.

Overlooked in the aftermath of his career, it's a long shot to hope that the Hall of Fame gives him a thorough second look once again almost fifty years since his passing. But if ever someone deserved such consideration, it's Stephens.

Chapter 7

LOCAL LEGENDS

The first local to reach the Major Leagues, Jack Rothrock, sort of slipped under the glove of the city, which was a bit of a shame, because the Poly product had a notable career that included being the first Major Leaguer to play all nine positions in a season, being a part of the most memorable World Series championship of the '30s, rooming with several Hall of Famers in his career and being manager of a minor league team that included Long Beach's scouting emeritus, Harry Minor.

"I knew Jack earlier because he was a Long Beach guy, but didn't know him well," said Minor, a standout ballplayer at Wilson whose career in professional baseball lasted six decades. "He was managing Anaheim [in the Sunset League] and got fired because the owner wanted a manager who could also play, and he came to us [in Riverside] in the middle of the year, and we won the league.

"He was quite a character, a tough SOB. There was no doubting he was a Gashouse Gang guy. He loved take-charge guys and never criticized anyone for being aggressive. He even drove the team bus at the end of the year. But he was really good with young kids. He never chewed you out. He'd come to the mound when I was pitching and tell me a little joke."

Rothrock, born in Long Beach in 1905, was a consummate baseball rat, playing ball wherever he could, including softball on a concrete field where he slid into bases with no regard for his legs. He played baseball and ran track at Poly from 1921 to 1923 but was ineligible his senior season because he played for a Bellflower semipro team in the summer.

Jack Rothrock (left), the first Long Beach native to play in the major leagues, sits on the bench at Wrigley Field in Los Angeles with teammate and another Poly High product, Jack Salveson.

Rothrock was writing a book on his career before he died in 1980 that included a passage about his days in Long Beach and the people and institutions that guided his young life: "The YMCA bible class under the direction of Gus Walker, and the camping trips guided by Milton Fish, then the Comus Club (at Poly) where I put on my first tuxedo and learned which side of the plate to place my knife and fork.

"Then Coach (Eddie) Kienholz of Poly High, who taught me to be a lousy loser and a good winner." The excerpt from Rothrock's unpublished book came from a story by Fresno sportswriter Scott Mayes, who interviewed Rothrock's widow Ardith Rothrock.

Rothrock signed with Arkansas City, a Class D team, after graduation in 1924 and finished the season with a .314 average. A Red Sox scout signed him in 1925, and he quickly made the jump to the majors.

He hit .347 in 22 games in 1925 and split 1926 with the Red Sox and their New Orleans farm team. He stuck in 1927, appearing in 117 games. His breakthrough came in 1928, when Red Sox manager Bill Carrigan, noting that Rothrock had played seven positions that season, decided to use him at the other two before season's end.

"He said I had done it all so far so I might as well pitch and catch before the season was over," Rothrock told the *Press-Telegram* in 1967. He threw a perfect 1-2-3 inning of relief on September 24 against Detroit and then started behind the plate and played an inning against Cleveland on September 29, making him the first Major Leaguer to play all nine positions in the same season.

Rothrock had his best season with the Red Sox in 1929, playing in 143 games and hitting .300 with twenty-four steals. An injury cut short 1930, but he returned a year later to hit .278 with eighty-one runs scored. But in the '30s, an era of power hitting, a singles hitter wasn't a big commodity. Boston traded him to the Chicago White Sox in 1932, and he spent half of the year in the minors. He was traded to the St. Louis Cardinals and got the attention of the Major League team in 1933 when he hit .347 for its Columbus farm team.

The 1934 Cardinals had more characters than the Disney movie vault. They quickly became known as the Gashouse Gang, a tag given them either by shortstop Leo Durocher or pitcher Dizzy Dean, depending on which story you believe. A "gashouse" was a plant, usually in a down-on-its-heels town, where coal was cooked and turned into gas, an environmentally unfriendly process that left towns and worker uniforms sooty and smelly.

The Cardinals—managed by Frankie Frisch and featuring Dean, his brother Paul, Durocher, Joe Medwick, Pepper Martin and Rip Collins—played baseball aggressively and literally wore their effort on their jerseys, which went unwashed on road trips.

Jack Rothrock (center) in a team picture taken at an old-timers game featuring the 1934 St. Louis Cardinals "Gashouse Gang."

In a 1967 *Press-Telegram* article, Rothrock said, "The team was cheap. We had one home and one road uniform. We went on a 14-day trip at the end of the season in New York and a writer said we looked like a Gashouse Gang."

The team was so cheap that it carried just twenty-one players, which explains why Rothrock played every inning of every game. "I had to play every day," he told the *St. Louis Globe Democrat* in 1980. "There wasn't anyone to take my place."

Rothrock, who writers said was the one gentleman on the team, said Pepper Martin embraced the name to a fault: "He'd wear the same pair of underwear for an entire road trip.

"We played a donkey baseball game once [where players ride donkeys around the bases] and Pepper decided to carry the donkey to first base instead of ride it. He liked to play practical jokes, and dropped a bucket of water from a high floor on [Frisch], who was wearing a brand-new white suit."

Rothrock would play a large role in the team's success, a ninety-five-win season that won the N.L. and then the World Series in seven games over Detroit. He led the league in games played (all 154), plate appearances and at-bats and ranked in the top ten in runs scored (106), doubles (thirty-five), steals and walks.

He hit .284 with career highs of eleven home runs and seventy-two RBIs. He hit second in the lineup behind Martin and became proficient in hitting the ball to right field to advance the ferocious Martin around the bases.

He contributed in all four wins by the Cardinals in the series. He had a two-run single in the second inning of Game 1 (a 7–3 win), scored a run and tripled in Game 3 (4–1), had two hits and a RBI in Game 6 (4–3) and doubled and scored to open the game in what became a Game 7 rout (11–0). He led the team in RBIs in the series with six.

He roomed with Red Ruffing during his early days with the Red Sox, long before Ruffing became a Hall of Fame pitcher with the Yankees. Ruffing and Rothrock would become lifelong friends. Rothrock worked as a civil engineer in the off-season and built Ruffing a house in Long Beach in 1937.

In 1935, his last season with the Cardinals, he was asked to play a tenth position—Hall of Fame babysitter. The Cardinals employed Grover Cleveland Alexander, the hero of their 1926 World Series win, in a modest capacity to help him through his drinking problems and roomed him with the reliable Rothrock.

He recalled one road trip where Alexander would walk from his bed or chair to a window and then stare out the window for a few minutes before walking back. Annoyed, Rothrock eventually looked at the window and saw a bottle of liquor in the sill, with a hospital feeding tube pinned to the drapes. Alexander had created his own discreet delivery system.

Rothrock spent 1936 in the minors and played in eighty-eight games for the 1937 Philadelphia A's. His contract was sold to the Los Angeles Angels of the Pacific Coast League, and he played with the Angels and Hollywood Stars from 1938 to 1940. In 1941, he had his last at-bat as a playing-manager in the minor leagues.

He spent the war years at home, holding a number of jobs before a stint with the navy's civil engineering unit, which included building cannon turrets along the coast from Long Beach to Palos Verdes. He owned a restaurant in the blossoming port area of Long Beach that he had to close because of the war needs, and his son recalled a day in the' 40s when he came home crying because he had just torn up a beautiful golf course on the ocean to install defense fixtures.

He returned to baseball in 1947, starting the season as manager of Anaheim in the Sunset League before being let go because the owner wanted a player-manager. He was quickly hired by Riverside and led the Dons to the league title. He'd manage three more years before retiring. He then moved to San Bernardino and worked in the parks department.

Rothrock died of a heart attack in 1980. As a young man, he told reporters in his rookie season that "he'd rather play ball than eat" and proved that by playing every position he could. As firsts go, you couldn't find someone more suited than Rothrock.

There's a postscript here. Two players with thin ties to Long Beach reached the majors before Rothrock—George Stovall and Zeb Terry—but those ties make string look like a bridge cable.

Stovall, a first baseman, was born in 1877, and his Major League career began in 1904. The late Poly historian Kenny Wooten found records of Stovall playing in three games for Poly in 1900, when he was twenty-three.

Terry, an infielder, was born in 1891 in Texas and reached the majors in 1916. A reference in his SABR bio says his family moved to California, and he graduated from Poly before attending Stanford beginning in 1910.

George "Firebrand" Stovall is included on several lists of former Long Beach Poly products, but he actually played for Poly before the era of organized high school baseball. He was in his twenties when he did so. He reportedly served as a coach at Poly in 1909 and later coached a semipro team in town. His brother Jesse was the manager of the 1913 Long Beach Beachcombers, one of the first pro teams in town.

In the early 1900s, there weren't a lot of rules regarding eligibility in high school sports. Long Beach High School—it became Poly years later—opened in 1895, and the first reference to a baseball team is 1899, when a semipro team donated old uniforms to the school team.

The CIF wasn't launched as an official entity until 1914. The CIF's own history is blunt about those early days: "The first organized interscholastic sports in Southern California started around the mid 1890's with no formalized organization or rules. High School Administrators took no part in these contests and anyone could play. Some of the players did not even attend the school and it was said that town bums were at times the coaches."

Stovall and Terry might have picked up a bat and ball in the name of Poly, but it was during an era where almost anyone in town could have done likewise. The two gentlemen are part of Long Beach's baseball lineage, but we'll stick with Rothrock as the "first."

In May 1961, Bob Bailey was finishing one of the finest high school baseball careers in CIF history, hitting .489 for the Bruins and setting the career record for hits in a Wilson career.

He would sign one of the biggest contracts in baseball history at the time, $150,000 with the Pittsburgh Pirates, and in 1962 began a seventeen-year Major League career.

It included two seasons with the hometown Dodgers (1967–68), a World Series ring as part of the 1976 Cincinnati Reds and a final 1978 season in Boston where the Red Sox lost a one-game A.L. playoff to Bucky F. Dent and the Yankees. He had his best seasons in the middle of his career with the Montreal Expos.

On its own merits, Bailey had a fine career. But the transition from high school star to Major Leaguer was a blueprint for what hype and circumstances can do to a prospect.

Bailey was heavily pursued in what would become the last of the bonus baby era, the pre-amateur draft era when all teams competed for prospects through signing bonuses. Major League baseball instituted the draft in 1965. The Tigers wanted him badly. Wilson alum Harry Minor worked Bailey and his dad, Buck, for the Braves. The Red Sox sent Ted Williams to Long Beach to sweet-talk Bailey. He eventually signed with Pittsburgh because the Pirates had pursued him steadily and Buck had a close friendship with Pirates scout Jerry Gardner.

"Dad had a loyalty to the Pirates scouting staff," Bailey told Doug Krikorian of the *Press-Telegram* on May 7, 1991. "One of their scouts had been his American Legion coach."

Instead of playing in intimate Tiger Stadium or in Boston with the Green Monster as a target, he would break in at Forbes Field, a cavernous ballpark that was not made for power-hitters.

"I don't have any regrets, but it was a big, big mistake," he said. "If I had to do it over again, I'd have signed with the Detroit Tigers. I'd have loved to hit at Tiger Stadium. Forbes was an airport, 406 feet to left field, 460 to center. Ridiculous. You'd hit a ball a mile, and it would be just one big out.

"It was bad for your confidence. I got real down on myself early in my career, and I think that hurt me. I got pretty frustrated during those four seasons in Pittsburgh."

He loved playing on a Pirates team managed by Danny Murtaugh and featuring Roberto Clemente. He thought coming to the Dodgers in 1967 would be a boon, but he came in a trade for the popular Maury Wills, who

Bob Bailey, with former major league outfielder Jim Piersall at a Long Beach Century Club banquet, signed for what was then a record $150,000 right out of Wilson by the Pittsburgh Pirates.

had clashed with management over a post-season playing tour and was quickly sent packing.

Bailey found his stride with the Expos, hitting more than twenty home runs and driving in more than eighty runs three times. The Reds acquired him as a reserve in 1976, and he hit .298 as a part-time left-fielder and pinch-hitter.

He finished his career with 187 home runs and was the first player to hit a home run in the upper deck at the Astrodome. He managed for several years after retiring.

Bob Bailey when he was a rookie with Pittsburgh.

"I honestly think the era in which I played in had the greatest array of baseball players ever—Mays, Mantle, Aaron, Clemente, Bench, Rose, Koufax, Morgan, Gibson, Seaver, Marichal, Cepeda, McCovey, Wills, Drysdale.

"You know what I miss most? Just playing the game of baseball,'" Bailey told Krikorian in a November 22, 2009 *Press-Telegram* column. "I loved it, every day of it. I knew it one day would end, but I used to not think about

Three of the top players to come out of Wilson High—Bobby Grich, Jeff Burroughs and Bob Bailey—share a moment in 1990.

it. Like life, I hoped it would go on forever...I look at myself as being very fortunate. How many people are fortunate enough to play in the majors as long as I did?"

Jeff Burroughs was the 1969 version of Bob Bailey. Like the Wilson third baseman, the Wilson outfielder was coming off a season as the CIF player of the year. Bailey was the premiere signing of 1961 in the pre-draft era. Burroughs was the first pick in the first round of the 1969 amateur draft, by the Washington Senators.

Like Bailey, he made his Major League debut in his second season of professional baseball. Bailey had a seventeen-year career to Burroughs's sixteen. Bailey played in a parking lot of a park with the Pirates, and Burroughs was a member of the last Washington Senators team in baseball history. Bailey met Ted Williams when the Red Sox tried to sign him out of high school. Burroughs played for Williams when he was a manager.

Burroughs's career was notable for winning the 1974 American League MVP Award, 240 career home runs and the kind of variety one could never imagine.

How many players can say they played in two games that ended in forfeits? Or had managers like Williams, and Billy Martin and Whitey Herzog before they were geniuses, and Wills during his controversial season-plus as a manager in Seattle and the one game in 1977 that Atlanta Braves owner Ted Turner decided to manage?

How many people could say they coached their own son—Sean, in Burroughs's case—to two Little League World Series titles and then saw his son also become a first-round draft pick in 1998?

Playing for Williams was a thrill because the Splendid Splinter was his idol when he was a kid. It was also an experience unlike any other that he, or anyone else, probably had with a manager.

"He was the loudest, most verbose man you'd ever meet," Burroughs said, noting that Williams had a hearing problem from his years flying in the Korean War. "He would talk to you as if you were 100 yards away, or at the far end of a five-bedroom house. And every other word was a cuss word. No one in history could cuss like that man, my God.

"Williams was a dead pull hitter, and he thought everyone should be. He used to say, 'You make history off the inside pitch.' And he considered pitchers to be the stupidest people in the world. He said all he had to do was pull one inside fastball, even if he hit it foul, to get pitchers to pitch him away, which is where he wanted to be pitched.

"He was very helpful to everybody. The problem was we just couldn't do it as well, because we weren't Ted Williams. He would get frustrated and say we had this God-given talent. He couldn't understand that we just weren't as good."

The Senators announced plans to relocate to Texas in 1971. Burroughs started in right field in the last game at RFK Stadium on September 30. The Senators were leading 7–5 in the top of the ninth when fans began running onto the field looking for souvenirs. A fan ran up on Burroughs and grabbed his hat, and within seconds, all of the Senator players were running for cover toward the dugout.

Fans grabbed the bases and were even trying to pry home plate from the round when the umpires called the game. "That was a sad way for a franchise to end," Burroughs said.

Burroughs would go through this again, "and that time, well, you really feared for your safety." On June 4, 1974, Burroughs was playing for the Texas Rangers when the attendance-starved Cleveland Indians hosted a ten-cent beer night promotion that turned ugly. During the course of the game, a fan threw a firecracker into the Rangers dugout and another threw a bottle at first baseman Mike Hargrove.

The game was tied 5–5 in the ninth when the drunken fans spilled onto the field, one running up on Burroughs as he was standing on second. Again, he and his teammates ran for cover, and the game was awarded to the Rangers via forfeit.

"We could tell by the fifth inning that things were getting out of control," he said. "They didn't have any extra police or security officers at the game."

All of the home runs and the MVP award and the oddities add up to a fine career, but Burroughs says nothing matched the excitement of being an assistant coach on the 1992 and 1993 Long Beach Little League World Series team that won back-to-back titles. The '92 team lost on the field but got the title on a bounce—the opponent used several ineligible players (see chapter 14). The 1993 team returned to Williamsport, including Sean, and won the title 3–2 in their last at-bat.

"It easily is the highlight of my baseball career," Burroughs said to Krikorian in a September 3, 1992 *Press-Telegram* column. "In my mind, nothing comes close to equaling it. To see what these kids accomplished under difficult circumstances was the topper for me.

"The way these kids hung in there at difficult moments brought tears to my eyes on more than one occasion. I'd been involved with the development of most of these kids since they were around five years old, and I'm just so darned proud of what they accomplished."

The Fairly family was well known in Long Beach long before Ron Fairly went from Jordan High to USC and to the Los Angeles Dodgers. His dad, Carl, played minor league baseball, and his brother Rusty was a standout football player at Denver University. Ron topped them with a whirlwind of success between 1956 and 1959.

He was the CIF player of the year in 1956, played on USC's 1958 College World Series championship team, broke into the majors the same year with the Los Angeles Dodgers and won a World Series ring in 1959. He added World Series appearances in 1963, 1965 and 1966 and spent twenty-one years in the majors.

Retired *Los Angeles Times* sportswriter Ross Newhan, who went to Wilson and began his writing career at the *Press-Telegram*, wrote that Fairly was the best high school baseball player he had ever seen. Fairly said the man who helped give his career shape was his dad.

"Like any dad he played with his sons," Fairly told Paul Hirsch for a bio as part of the SABR biography project in 2012. "We played catch; he gave me all the fundamentals and helped make me a ballplayer."

Ron Fairly was known as a baseball standout at Jordan High, the University of Southern California and with the Los Angeles Dodgers, but he was also a fine basketball player while at Jordan.

Fairly chose USC over UCLA even though he had a scholarship offer to play basketball for John Wooden and the Bruins. His first love was baseball, and one look at the ballparks of the two teams helped his decision—right field was a pasture at UCLA and cozy at USC's Bovard Field. At USC in '58, Fairly hit .348 with nine home runs and sixty-seven RBIs in 1958. He took less money from the Dodgers to play at home.

He played right away, making the team in September 1958. He was a youngster on the first two L.A. Dodger teams that were loaded with veterans from the Brooklyn era—Duke Snider, Gil Hodges, Carl Erskine, Carl Furillo and Pee Wee Reese.

"I learned a lot those two years, just about how you carry yourself as a major leaguer," Fairly told the *Press-Telegram* in 1963. "I got the chance to room with Snider for a few years and he taught me a lot. I got close with Furillo in 1959 and he helped teach me how to handle a ball off the wall."

Fairly became a regular in 1962 and was a large part of the Dodgers' '60s success. The Dodgers began to fray in 1967—Koufax retired after the '66 season—and Fairly was traded away to Montreal.

After more than eleven years of playing for a successful franchise, Fairly chafed with the low expectations of the expansion Expos. But he stayed a steady producer for another decade and became the first player to make the All-Star game for both Canadian franchises in baseball, the Expos and Blue Jays.

Fairly had a twenty-seven-year broadcasting career after his playing days and was well liked during his days with the Angels but grated on Bay Area fans when he joined the Giants' broadcast team. Once a Dodger, always a Dodger, and he finished his career in Seattle.

Poly had a foundational family tie in one baseball player. The Moffitts had a son and daughter who became stars in their respective sports—Randy, as

Randy Moffitt was a source of inspiration for his young sister, tennis star named Billie Jean King. He supported his sister's desire to play sports at a time when athletic opportunities for young women weren't plentiful.

a pitcher, and his sister, who became one of the greatest female athletes of all-time: Billie Jean King.

The two were inseparable as kids. Billie Jean went to Randy's games and longed to play sports. When she finally found tennis, Randy became her biggest supporter at a time when tennis executives weren't exactly treating women's tennis, or his sister, with much respect.

Randy forged a great career in baseball. He was a two-time all–Moore League choice at Poly and the team MVP of Long Beach's Connie Mack championship team of 1969, and he played at Long Beach State, where he won eighteen games in his two varsity seasons for coach Bob Wuesthoff and helped the school to its 1969 CCAA title.

In January 1970, the San Francisco Giants made him their first-round pick in the draft, and by 1972, he was in the majors. He was one of the top closers in the National League during the '70s, even though no one called them closers back then. Between 1973 and 1978, he averaged sixty-one appearances a year and posted seventy-seven saves, in an era when late-inning relief pitchers made more than one-inning cameos.

"I had a lot of two- and three-inning saves back then," he said. "We were just getting specialized, and guys were just starting to be recognized for what they did. Then it sort of exploded in the '80s."

He might have played longer if his body hadn't bailed on him, a situation that dogged him long after his playing days.

He came down with an infection in his stomach in 1979 that made eating extremely difficult and literally left him retching most every day. The source of the problem—a parasitic disease common to barnyard animals and one so rare that there were only one hundred recorded cases of it for humans—wasn't discovered until late 1980, so he went through two years of doctors and the Giants looking at him awkwardly .

"It was a rough time for him," his sister said. "To be getting that kind of put-down after nine years of good service. I was pretty upset."

He was able to deal with the malady and had one more good year in the majors. He won six games and had ten saves for Toronto in 1983. "I didn't overcome it as much as learn to live with it," he said. "Plus, by then my shoulder was hurting so bad that I realized I couldn't do this anymore, so I hung them up.

"Those were the 12 best years of my life. I loved it, every day of it. I loved to play."

Chapter 8

LONG BEACH'S CRADLE OF COACHES

A good baseball coach is a father figure, a role model, a teacher and anything else that might describe someone who leaves an imprint on a young athlete's life.

A coach spends his time teaching young kids about life through the lens of baseball, with its sacrifices and hit-and-runs and pick-off plays. A good coach makes himself available and does not curry favor, is as generous with a compliment as a criticism and will fight for his kids while maintaining integrity. A good coach who can explain the fine line between pride and arrogance is simply priceless.

Long Beach's baseball history may be written largely about the athletes, but it's necessary to note that not one of the greats would have reached the Major Leagues without good coaches. Long Beach's athletic heritage has largely been writ by coaches, most of them on the high school level.

Selecting just one baseball coach to summarize these greats would be unfair, but most everyone would agree where to start, with a coach who was once described thusly by Billy Witz of the Press-Telegram on May 24, 1998: "[He] is equal parts erudite and air bag, cantankerous and compassionate, scrupulous and scatter-brained. It's all right there, as plain to see as the mustard stain on his uniform."

He is John Herbold, and everyone who spent time in one of his dugouts would acknowledge all that and more. He chafed some, but those who came back for more were better off for the experience.

"The first person you come to always is Herbold," current Wilson coach Andy Hall said. "His legacy and impact in Long Beach is everywhere. I had the chance to play for him just once, and I'll never forget his love and zest for the game, and the way he made you feel about the game just by being with him."

One story neatly summarizes his zeal. He was coaching a Connie Mack game at Blair Field on the day Neil Armstrong strolled on the moon in 1969. The Eagle landed at 1:17 p.m., and a fellow youth coach in the stands yelled out to Herbold, "Hey John, we've just landed on the moon."

Herbold responded, "We've got a ballgame to win here."

John Herbold won 938 games in his forty-nine years as a head coach and is in four Hall of Fames—Long Beach Century Club, Cal State–Los Angeles, American Baseball Coaches Association and Hollywood High School. He was the head coach at Long Beach Poly from 1955 to 1968, dominating the Moore League and winning a CIF title in 1963 and getting to the title game in 1968.

He was head coach at Lakewood High from 1969 to 1983, winning thirteen Moore League titles and two more CIF titles (1970, 1974), and at Cal State–Los Angeles from 1984 to 2004. Even when he was coaching collegians, he was never far from Long Beach, be it through camps and clinics and just being around ballgames at Blair Field or wherever there was a diamond.

It has been estimated that three hundred of Herbold's players went on to play professionally. He personally estimates that Long Beach is the greatest baseball-producing city in the world.

"Baseball has been the main connection in my life for 60 years, and the best years have been in Long Beach," Herbold said in one of several interviews over the years. "Poly had fantastic athletes. The year we won CIF, it was part of a two-year period where the school won titles in baseball, football, basketball, track and golf. Lakewood probably has as many great ballplayers as any town."

Baseball people in Long Beach usually have one of two things to share about Herbold: a compliment or a story.

"Maybe it's just with my generation," Dan Peters, the former Millikan coach who played against him in the early '70s and coached against him in the '80s, said in the 1998 article. "But with all the baseball people in Long Beach, he's got to be one of the most influential in the city. I absolutely love the guy."

"He's the most influential and best coach or manager I've ever played for," Mike Fitzgerald, a catcher at Lakewood who had a ten-year Major League career, said. "If I had to play one game, I'd want John Herbold to manage it.

"If he had twenty-four hours to prepare against anybody, I'd bet on Herbold. He can motivate, encourage, scare players into paying attention. The game has changed now, of course, or the way you can coach has changed. But the team that wins is the team that throws strikes, plays good defense and hits the ball. That hasn't changed."

Herbold attended Hollywood High and was one of 110 kids trying out for the Bee baseball team, "and I was the first guy cut," he said. He persisted and eventually made the team as "a twerp, a 118-pound catcher on a team that finished last." His grades finished first. He qualified for Stanford and became infatuated with journalism, to the degree that he would later in life call up sportswriters to correct their grammar, which kept him busy.

"I actually wanted to go to Lehigh, but a neighbor had connections to Stanford, so I took the SAT late, passed, and he got me in," Herbold said. "The varsity usually carried three catchers. I was No. 4. I was always warming someone up. But I got in a few games, and the coaches always said I was like an extra coach."

After college—he was Phi Beta Kappa at Stanford and graduated in 1951 magna cum laude with a masters in journalism—Herbold went into the service, which is where he met two lifelong friends from Long Beach who would impact his career: Jack Teele, a former sportswriter at the *Press-Telegram* and executive with the Los Angeles Rams, and Bill Mulligan, a sports fanatic from Chicago who was a Poly football and basketball coach and later head basketball coach at the University of California–Irvine.

After the service, Herbold went looking for a high school teaching and coaching job with recommendations in hand from USC coaching legend Rod Dedeaux and Yankee owner Del Webb, who wrote a letter saying Herbold was good enough to manage the Yankees. "I knew Del's brother Marv," he said. "That was nice of [Del] even though I had never met him."

He was hired to teach and coach baseball at California High School in Whittier when Teele called to say Long Beach Poly was looking for a baseball coach. He interviewed, was offered the job and asked people who knew baseball which job he should take. "They all said if I wanted to coach the best talent, take the Poly job," he remembered.

He began teaching at Poly in 1955. His 1960 Poly team featured future Major Leaguers Tom Sisk and Ollie Brown, plus Willie Brown, who had a good career in football at Poly, USC and the NFL. His 1963 team won the CIF title, and the nucleus of that team would also win the American Legion title that summer.

In 1969, Herbold jumped to Lakewood High and the brand-new model city that had sprung up overnight north of Long Beach. In fifteen seasons, he won the Moore League title thirteen times and CIF titles in 1970 and 1976. He coached the Lancers to a record four straight CIF title games including 1976, losing three one-run games.

After fifteen years, he took the challenge of coaching Cal State–Los Angeles. "I didn't even know where Cal State L.A. was," Herbold said. He coached the Golden Eagles for twenty-one years, winning 455 games and getting the team into the 1998 NCAA Division II tournament. He remains a vibrant presence in the community, despite illness having kept him at home.

One of Herbold's favorite sayings is, "I treat all my players the same way—bad." But the truth is, he treated his players to his own fascination with baseball that, if they were lucky, came to fascinate them the same way.

The other baseball schools in town have a longer lineage of coaching icons. Al Johnson was Wilson's first baseball coach, and he handed the job to one of his former players, Cliff Meyer, who then handed it to one of his players, Skip Rowland. All three are eternally beloved by the Wilson family.

Al Johnson was a father figure to Wilson athletes from 1937 to 1967. As marvelous as his coaching career was, it was the way he reached out to student-athletes that made him unforgettable.

"Basically, he was a teacher," Rowland told the *Press-Telegram*'s Jim McCurdie in a September 4, 1997 story. "[Former UCLA basketball coach] John Wooden used to say that good coaching is good teaching, and [Johnson] was a fantastic teacher. Next to my father, I think he was the most influential figure in my life. And I think a lot of people would say the same thing."

Johnson was the head coach for Wilson's first-ever football league title in 1937, and six years later, he was the coach of the immortal "Jinxbusters" that posted the school's first-ever win over Poly. He called the 34–7 win the high point of his coaching career, mostly because of the impact it made on the community during World War II.

"It was during the war, and many mothers and dads swamped the Western Union office to send wires to their boys overseas," Johnson said in a 1983 interview with Loel Schrader of the *Press-Telegram*. "I got hundreds of wires from kids around the world congratulating us on the win."

Johnson spent just ten seasons as head football coach, winning six league titles and ten as baseball coach, and winning seven league crowns as well as the 1940 CIF title.

A meeting of Wilson baseball greats—Skip Rowland, Al Johnson, Bob Lemon and Eddie Bockman—at a Long Beach Century Club banquet.

Bob Lemon said Johnson was partly responsible for helping him realize his potential. "He was quite instrumental in straightening me out. I wasn't eligible for baseball my first year," Lemon told the *Press-Telegram*'s McCurdie. "I ditched a lot. I liked to play golf and fool around. Nothing malicious. Coach just gave me a different outlook on life.

"He was just a great, down-to-earth man. He took you serious, wanted to hear what you had to say. He made you feel wanted."

When Johnson stepped down as baseball's head coach, he handed the job to Meyer, who was the team captain of Wilson's first-ever football team and an assistant coach on the "Jinxbusters."

In Meyer's fifteen-year stint as head coach (1947–61), he won two CIF titles, reached the finals in another and coached four CIF players of the year—Vance Thurston, Frank Followell, Bud Daley and Bob Bailey. He was a different kind of coach, perhaps the antithesis of Herbold.

"Cliff hadn't coached too much baseball, so he said, 'Well, I'll let you do your thing,'" said Thurston, the star pitcher on the 1947 title team. "We

Cliff Meyer led Wilson High to CIF baseball titles in 1947 and 1950.

went out and won CIF and then we beat Fremont, the L.A. City champ. He'd have the whole team over to the house. Everybody loved him."

"I became a coach and an educator because of Cliff," said Buck Taylor, a pitcher on the 1950 title team who played at Long Beach City College and was a baseball coach and athletic director at Warren High for thirty-four years. "His greatest strength was adjusting what he did to the young men and women he coached and taught."

Meyer also launched three generations of Meyers who served Long Beach sports and education. His son Jon was a former Wilson coach and principal at Lakewood, and Jon's son Scott was the head football coach at Jordan and recently won back-to-back CIF football titles at Corona Del Mar.

The program stayed in the hands of Wilson products after Meyer was transferred from Wilson to Jordan. Skip Rowland's legacy included playing football and baseball at Wilson—he played on the "Jinxbusters"—and spent thirty-five years at the school as a coach and teacher. That didn't include another twenty-five years as a supporter and fundraiser for the school's athletic programs.

From 1951 to 1988, save for two years in the '50s, he was a head coach or assistant at Wilson in multiple sports. More importantly than any games or titles he won, he was a fixture for hundreds of young men who say their success on or off the field had a lot to do with the lessons learned from Rowland.

Bobby Grich, the former Angels standout second baseman, played football and baseball for Wilson, and recalls one moment with Skip that had a huge impact on his Major League career.

"My senior year, Bill Crutchfield was the baseball coach and Skip was an assistant, but he took over for a day or two when Bill had something to do," Grich said. "I was in the cage and Skip was hanging on it, and after a few swings,

Skip Rowland.

he says, 'Wait on the ball, then go pop. Wait, wait, wait, then pop.' No one had ever told me that. It sounded counter-productive.

"But once I did it, it clicked right away. It allowed me to keep my left shoulder in and not step out too soon, and it's something I remembered throughout my career. Here Skip comes out for a cameo appearance with baseball, says something very simple that took maybe thirty seconds, and I remembered it for twenty years. He was always a voice on my shoulder."

"I got to know Skip my first year," Hall, who led Wilson to its first title in fifty-seven years in 2007, said. "I always knew what he meant to the school, but watching the way kids responded to him, his presence, on my first day, was very special.

"Whatever pressure I've felt [as Wilson coach] has mostly been self-inflicted. But there's no denying the history that exists in the program and the examples that people like Cliff and Skip set. It becomes an unspoken part of the job that you want to maintain that tradition."

Lakewood opened in 1956, and fifty-seven years later, it has had just three baseball coaches, Artie Boyd, Herbold and Spud O'Neil, and the cumulative run of success has separated the Lancers from the rest of the Moore League.

Boyd's Lakewood success was an extension of the Wilson family tree. He was a third baseman on Meyer's 1947 CIF title team, then starred at Long Beach City College for two years and Arizona before launching a thirty-five-year career in the Long Beach Unified system. He was the first coach hired at Lakewood and won a CIF title in the school's sixth year. He stayed at Lakewood through 1968 and would later coach at Poly (1971–73) and Millikan (1976–81).

Boyd won Lakewood's first title and Herbold cemented his legacy at Lakewood, but O'Neil has created a towering persona since becoming head

The troika of Lakewood High baseball coaches—Artie Boyd, John Herbold and Spud O'Neil.

coach for the Lancers in 1984. He has over seven hundred wins in his career, which includes five years as head coach at his alma mater, St. Anthony, and another five at Colton High.

Since 1984, O'Neil has led Lakewood to twenty Moore League titles, two CIF championships (1987, 2006) and the finals two other times. His Lancers have missed the postseason just once, and more than half of the Major League players produced by Lakewood played for O'Neil.

O'Neil's formula is steeped in fundamentals, and that includes surrounding himself with good assistant coaches who help keep the players on track year-round. Lakewood's American Legion teams have always been of the highest caliber—they won state and regional titles in 2012—and the Lancers work closely with the feeder programs at the area's numerous PONY, Colt and Connie Mack leagues.

"We have a great Pony-Colt feeder program out of Heartwell Park, and baseball in Lakewood is very competitive from a young age," O'Neil said. "We've had a lot of success. I always tell the kids to enjoy this, because it's so hard just getting to the top. People expect us to be successful. But I expect that, too."

"Spud taught me so much and really let me grow as a coach," Rob Wigod, now the commissioner of the CIF-Southern Section, said when he was the head baseball coach at Los Alamitos High. "A lot of head coaches don't give their assistants as much responsibility as I had [at Lakewood], and that is to his credit."

A 1965 graduate of St. Anthony, Walter O'Neil played football, basketball and baseball for the Saints and went to Long Beach City College and Long Beach State. In-between, he did an army hitch that included a one-year stay in Vietnam. He always knew he wanted to coach and had his first head coaching job before he was thirty. He has no aspirations to retire any time soon, either. "The kids keep me young," he says.

Millikan often lies in the shadows of Wilson and Lakewood, yet between 1967 and 2001, the Rams won five CIF titles and went to the title game four other times. The coaches for those teams were Bob Myers and Dan Peters.

Like Boyd at Lakewood, Bob Myers was the first-ever coach at Millikan. He had spent three years in the marines and five years playing minor league baseball before becoming a Long Beach Unified teacher in 1953. He won 184 games between 1956 and 1969, including CIF titles in 1967 and 1969. That 1969 team included a third baseman named Dan Peters, future Angels pitcher Dave Frost and a roster that doubled up that summer to win an American Legion title.

Dan Peters followed Bob Myers at Millikan and led the Rams to three CIF titles.

Myers decided to move to the college ranks in 1970 and was an assistant for Joe Hicks at Long Beach City College for several years until succeeding him in 1976. He was the Vikings head coach for six years, won 170 games, three conference titles and the 1976 state championship.

Peters played for Myers at Millikan and then Hicks at LBCC and even played a year of basketball for Lute Olson. He played at Cal State–Fullerton when Augie Garrido was head coach and future Long Beach State coach Dave Snow was an assistant, and Peters's roommate was George Horton. The '75 Titans won the College World Series title.

He immediately went into coaching as an assistant at LBCC for two years, and three years later, he returned to his alma mater in 1984. He stayed for twenty-three seasons, won 507 games as head coach and posted the most wins of any CIF-SS school during the decade of the '90s (217).

Peter's teams reached the title game seven times and won three titles, in 1983 and back-to-back titles in 1991-92, the first school to win consecutive titles since Chaffey High won three in 1956–58.

In all but one of Millikan's title game appearances, the team came into the postseason as an underdog. Only once did they win the Moore League and parlay it into a title shot. They snuck up on teams but won because they were fundamentally solid.

"We're so close to Lakewood and Wilson so the pool of talent is well-stocked," Peters said before the 2001 title game. "When kids come here, we try to create an environment where they can get the most of their ability. The kids all know each other, so it's a competitive situation.

"One of the top [thrills] for me…was having some of my former players return to the school to coach for me," Peters said in a June 2004 story by James Melroy in the *Press-Telegram.* "It's kind of a validation of what I was trying to do during my time there, that I've had some kind of impact on them. When they're coming back to the program and wanting to be a part of it, that feels pretty special."

There is little one can add to a man's baseball resume when it includes this fact: Joe Hicks was buried with a baseball in his hand.

When the Long Beach City College baseball coach for more than twenty-five years (1950–75) passed away from colon cancer in 1991, his wife, Joyce, saw to it that he went to heaven with something he loved.

Hicks had as much impact on young men as the great high school coaches. He just did it in two-year parcels at the community college level, and LBCC was around for decades before Long Beach State came along in 1949.

In his twenty-six seasons, he won 513 games, three state titles, seven Southern California titles and thirteen conference championships. More than one hundred former Vikings who played for Hicks went on to play professionally. He was also a full-time teacher on campus in physical education.

Joe Hicks was Long Beach City College's football coach during the winter and baseball coach in the spring.

Hicks was a multisport athlete at Banning High, pitched at UCLA and spent two years in the St. Louis Browns organization before starting his coaching and teaching career at LBCC.

He was always a teacher. He began recording his players with eight-millimeter cameras and would screen the video in his den. He devised an early version of the batting tee in the '50s and produced and marketed his own training films for athletes.

"He was a missionary, always spreading the baseball word," Herbold told Loel Schrader in a 1992 *Press-Telegram* story. "I said when he died that he knew more baseball than anyone I'd ever known. His given first name was 'Joe' but it really should have been 'Baseball.'"

"What I remember most about my father was that he cared about teaching and the profession of baseball, and that he was a real strong family man," his son Tom Hicks told Schrader. "And he really loved Long Beach. He felt it was a great honor to coach at Long Beach City College."

Hicks, a rugged-looking man, had a shadow career as an actor. He started picking up extra work in the late '40s. He was the double for actor Ray Milland in the baseball scenes of *It Happens Every Spring* and was the hitter in the scene of *The Dizzy Dean Story* where Dean is hit by a line drive.

He picked up parts in movies featuring Ronald Reagan, Elvis Presley, John Wayne, Charlton Heston and even James Dean (*East of Eden*). He had guest appearances in TV shows including *Gomer Pyle, USMC*; *Mr. Ed*; *The Untouchables*; *The Twilight Zone*; *The Lucille Ball Show* and *The Fugitive*.

In the mid-'60s, he appeared as the Marlboro Man in TV and print ads. "It was just something he did to help provide for his family," said Tom Hicks in a 1992 *Los Angeles Times* interview with Dick Wagner. "I remember he came home once and said, 'I had a tough day at the studio. I got killed seven times.'"

In his last season, his sons, Jay and Tom, were the pitcher and catcher for his 500th career win. He retired from coaching so he could follow their college careers. In 1977, he started Diamond Sports Inc. in Los Alamitos, a major supplier of athletic goods, which his son Jay eventually ran. Tom, meanwhile, went on to win a national title at USC and have his own college coaching career before becoming a private tutor.

Chapter 9

SNOWMAN

The logical title of this chapter should be "Dirtbags" or some kind of word play about a baseball program that produced dirty, sweaty, hungry young college ballplayers who wore their work on their uniforms like coal miners wore soot. "Gashouse Gang" star Jack Rothrock, the first local to reach the majors, would have loved the Dirtbags.

But truly, there wouldn't have been any Dirtbags at Long Beach State if not for head coach Dave Snow. The marketing campaign that turned the unofficial nickname into a nationally known and admired team would never have happened.

"Dirtbag baseball" became synonymous with nose-to-the-dirt baseball, an underdog mentality with a fascinating attention to detail, and while that was true, it was all Snow's doing. It was his coaching philosophy and his ability to find players who fit his style of play—or players he could get to fit—that made the program what it became. That it was wrapped up in a slightly off-color one-word nickname just made it easier to explain.

Long Beach State baseball soared to heights no one ever imagined because of Snow. The program had never been fully funded as a Division I program, and in 1988, it finished 16–41–1 and had a team ERA of 7.01.

Snow's first team in 1989 was put together hastily with spackle and hustle and won its first eighteen games, a school record fifty on the season and advanced to the College World Series for the first time. It remains the biggest one-season turnaround in college history.

Dave Snow, the coach who came in and reshaped the Long Beach State program in 1989.

In his thirteen seasons, Snow was 511–290–4 and took four teams to the College World Series and eleven to the postseason. Snow's teams won thirty-nine postseason games, all either on a neutral field or someone's home park. It took until 2003, but the program finally hosted a home NCAA regional and has done so five times to date.

And while it was never Snow's intention to become a feeder school for Major League Baseball, that's what Long Beach State has become. Thirty-seven players since Snow's first season have reached the majors, and in 2010, 2011 and 2012, the school had more players make an appearance than any other university.

In a memorable interview in 1996, he was asked if he was proud to send players to the majors. Snow quietly sent a spray of chewing tobacco skyward before clearing his throat and calmly saying, "We're here to win games."

At its most basic, that's what Dirtbag baseball has really been about.

"We tried to do everything right," he said. "There were no guarantees, but we would be thorough and focus on what it takes to put people in a position to win. There were a lot of good by-products from that, but the main mission was to win."

There was no "Dirtbag" profile. "It's a good question," he said. "I don't think we had to have a guy who fit a profile. It was more of a balancing act between looking for talent and makeup and then putting that player in a certain environment. There are a lot of players who have good qualities who can't tap into that.

"We recruited guys who had desire and a good makeup who had the potential to be a Dirtbag. Sometimes those guys stand out; they're grinders. Other times, it's a process of bringing those characteristics out. The player has to trust in himself, the coaches and the environment, which was all about structure and discipline."

Snow's philosophy was a direct connection to what he learned playing for Wally Kincaid at Cerritos College. After playing at Bellflower High, Snow became a two-year starter at Cerritos and in 1970 was the third baseman and team captain on a team that went 40–1 and won a state title.

A pensive moment for Dave Snow in the Dirtbag dugout.

Snow is still bothered about that one loss, which came in the second game of a doubleheader against San Diego City College after twenty-seven wins to open the season. The 1966 Cerritos team went 40–0, still the only California community college team to ever go unbeaten.

"We were 40–1 and disappointed," Snow said. "We wanted to be the best team he ever coached. We had pretty high standards."

Snow played two seasons at Cal Poly San Luis Obispo and was planning a pro career before an injury in his senior season turned his attention to coaching. In quick order, he became the head coach at L.A. Valley College and won a state title; became head coach at Loyola Marymount and took the Lions to the College World Series; and then was offered the Long Beach State job.

He took it because Loyola was wavering on its financial commitment to baseball, and its rules—high academics, no physical education major, a reluctance to take JC kids—gave him a smaller pool of players to recruit.

Long Beach State had never treated baseball with any urgency. It was a Division I school with no budget, a rickety home field and ten losing seasons in twelve through 1988. Then 49er athletic director Corey Johnson, who took the job with a promise that sports would become a priority, hired Snow and gave him the money necessary to recruit.

"I was like a kid in a candy store," he said. "I had all this scholarship money and could go after so many kids that I never could have recruited at Loyola." But he was building a team after most of the top players had already committed to other schools.

"I was so totally involved in the process of putting a team together that I didn't have the time to think about where we were headed," he said. "We were just trying to find ballplayers."

He got three transfers from Cerritos, where close friend George Horton was the head coach, including outfielder Darrell Sherman, who already had an offer from Cal State–Fullerton. Snow got pitcher Kyle Abbott, who was looking to transfer to a D-I school after starring at D-III UC San Diego. Snow found Andy Croghan, who was JC bound, pitching in a Connie Mack game.

Tom Urbani was recommended by a colleague as an outfielder; Snow turned him into a pitcher. Cerritos transfer Toby Sanchez was a 140-pound outfielder; Snow made him a catcher. Chris Gill, one of the few holdovers from 1988, was a switch-hitter when Snow arrived. Snow got him to hit just from the right side, and his average soared. Snow also hired Kincaid as an assistant coach, having the man who helped launch his career at his side.

Don Barbara was one of the original members of the 1989 Dirtbags. *Courtesy Long Beach State.*

Don Barbara had wanted to play for Snow at Loyola, but there were no scholarships available. A few months later, Snow called and asked him to come to Long Beach.

"It was a dream," he said. "There were no expectations and we had a coach who had gone to the College World Series. We were a bunch of guys who had no place to go and were always moving from one field to the next, and so we did a lot of things together as a team.

"Then we won our first 18 games. It was unreal."

Snow's goal was to win, but he realized there was something unique about that first team that stuck with the program.

"A big part of baseball to me is attitude and mental toughness," he said. "If anything came out of [1989], it was realizing we didn't have much—no home field, guys other schools didn't want or take. So our attitude was 'bring it on.' Whatever adversity we had to deal with we managed to overcome. We developed a toughness to have success in the face of failure. That's what was so special. Guys wanted to get in the arena and battle."

What made it special to Barbara was Snow's perspective: "He taught you a lot. He wanted you to be self-motivated, and to buy-in to what he wanted, doing all of those little things."

In 1989, that included finding a place to play and practice. The campus field was getting a new irrigation system, so the team had to play its home games elsewhere, most often at Long Beach City College or Cerritos College.

Practice was a daily coin flip. The team often split into groups and headed to different fields. Assistant coach Dave Malpass worked with the infielders and often found himself driving the team's equipment to a PONY League field at Whaley Park that was either rock-hard and dusty from a lack of watering or a mud pit after a rainstorm.

Malpass got used to ending each day gazing at uniforms that were caked in either dirt or mud, as well as players who had picked up a few bruises. "If somebody got a bad hop and got hit, they weren't going to let everybody know they didn't want the next ball. It had to do with mental toughness as much as anything else," he said to Billy Witz in a 1997 *Press-Telegram* story.

One day, he looked at his players and a name was born. He said, "You guys look like a bunch of Dirtbags."

"Alan Burke had a chipped tooth from a bad hop, but after awhile we kind of came to love it," Barbara said. "We wanted to take the bad hops and get hit and get tougher. The first time coach used the word 'Dirtbags,' it stuck like the dirt. It's how we referred to ourselves."

The 1989 team won its first Big West title and advanced to the College World Series, where their rags-to-riches story won admirers. Two years later, Snow's team, led by Jason Giambi and Steve Trachsel, won its regional at Austin, Texas, and impressed the Longhorn fans so much that the crowd of three thousand serenaded the Dirtbags after the title game win, singing the school fight song and flashing the Hook 'Em Horns hand signs. They advanced to Omaha, survived a tornado warning and won a game before being eliminated.

The 1993 team is a landmark in Snow's tenure, one of his favorite teams but also one of his most difficult. That was the first year the team made Blair Field its home, and with that came a little sense of comfort unusual to the program. The team was inconsistent early and sitting at 13–12 before a trip to New Mexico State. After two sloppy wins, the Dirtbags gave the third game of the series away.

Jeff Liefer, who was in his freshman season of a great college career that would send him to the majors, remembers Snow getting so upset in the last game in New Mexico that he stopped coaching. "He was upset," Liefer said. "He wasn't even sending any signals to the coaches or catchers. We then got upset with him, feeling like he had quit on us."

The next day, a 6:00 a.m. practice was called—not on the field, but on the campus track. Snow ran them.

"That was a confrontational point," Snow said. "From a military viewpoint, I had tried to break them down and in the process I almost lost them." Snow's message, though, was clear—you didn't become a Dirtbag just by being on the team, and the coach was willing to do whatever it took to get that point across.

"I'm not sure we really understood that until the end of the season, when we saw the way things played out," Liefer said. "We needed to buy-in to what he wanted, and we would only be successful if we did."

The 1993 team proceeded to go 28–4 the rest of the season, including 15 straight wins at one point and an unbeaten regional that sent them back to Omaha. There, they came three outs away from playing for the national title, taking a 5–3 lead into the ninth against LSU before the eventual champs rallied for three.

"I came to Long Beach because I loved the city and loved the kind of baseball the team played,'" Liefer said. "I wanted to play baseball there. I was a competitive player, but Coach Snow is the one who really gave me the tools to succeed. I learned there was more to baseball than the three-run home run.

"There were times when he almost seemed to will the talent out of you just by being so determined that you fulfilled your ability and was committed to the team."

"The thing about the '93 team is that they trusted me and hung through it, and they became very tough men in the process," Snow said. "They came through as much adversity as any of my teams."

The 1993 season was pivotal in so many respects. It showed that the team was more than just a colorful nickname. It cemented the program's national

The Dirtbag bench erupts after Long Beach State finishes its win over LSU in the 1993 college World Series.

appeal. Making Blair Field home gave the program substance. And suddenly, players were pursuing the Dirtbags, and the pros were pursuing them. Ten players were drafted off the 1993 team. Liefer was a first-round pick in 1995.

The 1994 team won forty-one games, the 1995 team came a misplayed bunt away from a trip to Omaha and the 1997 team pushed LSU to the brink again in the regionals. The 1998 team, led by a powerful lineup and bolstered by Mike Gallo's pitching down the stretch, started 2–8–1 and then went 35–12 to get to the regionals, knocked out No. 3 Stanford on its home field and finished third in the CWS, behind national champ USC and runner-up Arizona State.

"A lot of things came to fruition in 1993," Snow said. "The Dirtbag thing took on its own life and [former LBS marketing director] John Costello took it into new areas. Now it was a term associated with the program in great regard, more than just something internal.

"Where the program went speaks to the worth ethic, the coaching, and the fruits of the labor. Seeing players want to play for us was satisfying, but the emphasis always stayed on the process, not the product."

Snow coached three more seasons and then surprised a lot of friends by deciding to retire. His top assistant, Mike Weathers, took over in 2002, sparked new firsts and increased the high-end recruiting success of previous seasons. In 2002, the Dirtbags eliminated Fullerton from the NCAA regionals. In 2003, Long Beach hosted its own regional. In 2004, perhaps the best team in school history upset Stanford in Palo Alto in the regionals and hosted a super regional at Blair.

Leading 5–2 in the ninth in Game 1 against Arizona, Jered Weaver exited after 137 pitches and the bullpen couldn't cap an Arizona rally. The Dirtbags won Game 2, then dropped Game 3 4–3 in eleven innings on an unearned run.

It would be wrong to say the program never recovered from that loss, but it definitely lingered. The Dirtbags hosted three more regionals but were eliminated in each one. By then, there were a lot of college baseball teams playing the same kind of baseball Dave Snow brought to Long Beach.

The program hasn't been to the postseason since 2008. Troy Buckley's three teams have straddled .500 while trying to regain whatever mojo the Dirtbag name has lost. The team has lost several high-profile recruits to the MLB draft, but it also hasn't had a high profile bat since Danny Espinosa and Shane Peterson in 2008, and Peterson was recruited as a pitcher.

What's mostly been lost is that thing Snow always sought—players who buy in 100 percent to the type of play and discipline he wanted. There's been a lot of players excited to be a Dirtbag but very few with the discipline and commitment to play like one.

"We were orphans," Chris Gill told Billy Witz of the *Press-Telegram* in 1997. "A lot of the guys nobody wanted. If there was ever a definition of overachievers, we were it. No way in hell we should have been going to the College World Series."

Chapter 10

THE DIRTBAG LEGACY

When the 1989 season began, Long Beach State had sent a total of six players to the Major Leagues, with only one, Randy Moffitt, having a long career, and another, Dick Nen, had a kismet moment with the Dodgers.

Over the next twenty-four years, from 1989 to 2013, thirty-seven members of the Dirtbags have advanced to the majors. In the last three years (2010–12), Long Beach led all collegiate programs with the most players who played in the majors those seasons.

Evan Longoria came to Long Beach State a thin third baseman and blossomed into an American League All-Star. *Courtesy Long Beach State.*

Jason Giambi, the 2000 A.L. MVP, is in his eighteenth season. Steve Trachsel played sixteen seasons and was the first product to play in an All-Star game. Chris Gomez had a sixteen-year career that included a World Series appearance in 1998. Bobby Crosby was the A.L.'s Rookie of the Year in 2003.

Two-thirds of the players who reached the majors played four to eight years in the pros, including active players like Marco Estrada, Jason Vargas and Danny Espinosa.

And three players are among the best in baseball at the time of this writing: pitcher Jered Weaver (Angels), shortstop Troy Tulowitzki (Rockies) and third baseman Evan Longoria (Rays).

When Jason Giambi was five, his father, John, put a bat in his hands and told him it would be his path in baseball. "Dad told me, 'If you can hit, they'll always find a place for you to play. They'll always put you somewhere,'" Giambi said in a 1992 *Press-Telegram* article. Giambi found his place in baseball, but the story goes beyond that one moment. By the time he was ten, he had a poster that Ted Williams made famous on the cover of his book. It is a rectangle of the strike zone filled with eleven rows of seven baseballs (seventy-seven total), each labeled with the batting average that Williams projected for hitting a ball in that part of the strike zone.

It was a great learning device. Chase that low-and-away pitch, and you'll be fortunate to hit .250. There's a sweet spot low and inside, but it's small. Giambi memorized it. "When I was 10 to 12 years old, my dad would throw

When he first arrived at Long Beach State, Jason Giambi was a thin third baseman. *Courtesy Long Beach State.*

pitches to me and I would have to tell him where it was on the chart and what the average was when I hit it," Giambi said in 1992.

By the time he was in high school, he was taking batting practice seven days a week in the cage his dad built in their West Covina home. Such are the vagaries of baseball that Jason Giambi had a good South Hills High school career, but the school he wanted to attend, USC, didn't offer him a scholarship.

One school did. Dave Snow saw all of the hitting upside. He also could see that Giambi was a player without position but believed he could be taught if he had the same drive that he did as a hitter.

Giambi turned into a credible college third baseman and a solid Major League first baseman. He played more games at first than any other position and didn't start filling a DH role until he was thirty-four.

"Dave Snow had a tremendous impact on me as a player," he said. "I didn't have any other scholarship offers, anywhere else to go. He came to me, and I had to try out for him, but he ended up giving me a partial scholarship. He really got me focused. I was already a student of the game, but he was on it every day. He didn't accept mistakes.

"We were the Dirtbags. We were the guys nobody else wanted, and before you know it, we were winning, going to the College World Series. We were all like diamonds in the rough. Most of the guys he coached have gone on to good [pro] careers. He's a tremendous baseball man, as far as transforming guys into real ballplayers."

In his three seasons as a Dirtbag, Giambi hit .397, which is third all-time behind Don Barbara's .420. He had two seasons hitting over .400, a .506 on-base percentage and 125 RBIs.

He finished his eighteenth season in the majors in 2012, with a career line of .280/.403/.522, 429 home runs and 1,405 RBIs. He spent eight seasons in Oakland, became the face of the franchise after Mark McGwire's departure and won the 2000 A.L. MVP award for a .342/.477/.660 line and career-high forty-three home runs and 137 RBIs. He was the runner-up in 2001.

He spent the next seven seasons in New York and basically matched his numbers in Oakland, except in 2004. That was the year he began to feel debilitating fatigue, the result of an intestinal parasite and a benign pituitary tumor. All of his numbers fell off the side of the earth.

That was also the year that the *San Francisco Chronicle* uncovered his 2003 deposition before a federal grand jury on the BALCO steroid scandal. His name had already been linked to BALCO; what people didn't know is that when questioned, he admitted to using steroids and human growth hormone from 2001 to 2003. Before the 2005 season began, Giambi publicly apologized.

He was criticized, but he truly was the antithesis of what everyone else involved in baseball did or would do when steroid use came up. Rafael Palmeiro was defiant in his denials—before testing positive. Sammy Sosa spoke like he didn't know what steroids were. Barry Bonds was nonchalant and stoic. Roger Clemens arrogantly attacked anyone who accused him.

Giambi admitted the truth and went back to playing baseball.

"[That was] probably the toughest year in my big-league career, trying to come back from everything," he said. When asked if he was bothered by the criticism, he said, "I don't really care what anybody thinks. I know what I have done…so it doesn't matter what anyone says. Fans like to be skeptical. Some people want to hate and beat you up and keep you down. I'm not going to let that happen to me."

His illness was buried under the avalanche of criticism. "Nobody wants to remember that I was sick," he said. "The tumor was in the one place that controls the whole body. I hurt everywhere. I was exhausted. I couldn't sleep. I probably shouldn't have tried to play, but I wanted to try and help the team."

He took heart from the support of those closest to him. The Dirtbag community remained behind him.

"They've always been good to me, the Dirtbag fans and the whole Long Beach State community…Anytime I go back, I'm made to feel more welcome than I probably deserve."

In 2005, he bounced back with a 32-homer, 87-RBI season and followed that in '06 with 37 and 113. He is tested every year for steroids and other banned substances as a result of his admission, and he always comes back clean.

"I wasn't surprised one bit by the way he came back," said Don Barbara, one of the original Dirtbags and a teammate in 1990. "He was always a pure hitter. You can talk about steroids, you can talk about what steroids can do for you, but they had nothing to do with his ability to hit and get on base all the time. He's been able to drive in runs since he was in high school."

The 2013 season is Giambi's nineteenth in baseball, and it's a statement on his career arc that he's gone from being a young pup in Oakland to an elder statesman with the Rockies the last few years and now in Cleveland. Years after his dad put a bat in his hand, Giambi is still making contact.

No one had to ask Troy Tulowitzki twice if he wanted to be a Dirtbag. Out of all the players recruited by Dave Snow and Mike Weathers who fit the ideal of the nose-in-the-dirt style, Tulowitzki is the model. He is a one-man electrical storm; he was like that in high school, college and in a pro career already touched by greatness.

Tulowitzki's dad, Ken, started playing catch and sticking a bat in Troy's hands when he was a toddler. His father coached him through youth baseball and into high school at Fremont High in Sunnyvale.

"I was a baseball guy," Tulowitzki said, "from the age of two on. Some guys get tired of playing at a certain age. But as soon as I caught on, I never wanted to stop. I love playing. I can't imagine not playing. The flow of baseball is contagious. If you love it as much as I do, you never want to get out of that flow."

Tulowitzki was recruited out of high school by several Division I programs, including Fullerton, Baylor and Santa Clara, but he went undrafted because he wasn't close to filling out his current six-foot-three, 210-pound frame. When it came time to pick a college, it wasn't hard for him to realize where he wanted to play in college.

"When I read the blurb in the media guide about what a Dirtbag was, it fit," he said. "The philosophy here is a lot like what I learned from Dad, good defense, play hard, fundamentals, team play.

"It was the best choice I ever made. The coaches were great. The camaraderie on the team was great. I'll do anything to help Long Beach State in its recruiting because I honestly think it's the best place for a young player to attend. It's what you want as a college player. The team has a reputation for playing the right kind of baseball.

"The fans and atmosphere around the program are fantastic. There are so many people I've met over the years who are just fans. They don't have kids playing on the team. They're just Dirtbag fans, and they become your friends and part of your family."

Tulowitzki played from 2003 to 2005 and hit .310 with twenty home runs and 117 RBIs. He led the team in RBIs as a freshman, in home runs in the 2004 season on what may have been the most talented Long Beach team and in homers and average in 2005. His playing time was cut a bit by a hamate bone injury in 2005.

He was the seventh pick by Colorado in the 2005 draft, and late in 2006, he was recalled by the Rockies. By the middle of his first full season in the minors, he was recalled by Colorado, the quickest jump from Blair Field to the majors of any Dirtbag ever.

Tulowitzki may go down in history as one of the best all-around shortstops of the modern era, a rare player with power and fielding prowess. *Courtesy Long Beach State.*

The 2013 season will be Tulowitzki's eighth. He hit .291 with twenty-four home runs, ninety-nine RBIs and jaw-dropping defense in 2007 and was runner-up to Ryan Braun in the Rookie of the Year voting. He might have won the award if voting hadn't ended with the regular season. Tulo was a key factor in Colorado's run to the World Series. The Rockies won thirteen of their last fourteen to close a five-and-a-half-game deficit in the standings and then beat San Diego in eleven innings in a one-game playoff for the N.L. wild card.

The Rockies then won seven more straight games, sweeping Philadelphia in the NLDS and Arizona in the NLCS to reach the World Series, where they were finally stopped by Boston.

He has had three amazing seasons since then, the 2009–2011 arc where he hit eighty-nine home runs and 292 RBIs and hit .310. The only bumps have been seasons slowed by injuries (2008 and 2012). In the course of 2007, he became a team leader on a young team and remains that today, oddly now a veteran even though he's just twenty-eight.

"I knew Tulo was very capable, but I never thought he'd do so well so soon," Weathers said. "On the offensive side, I thought it would take him a while to figure it all out. But Tulo is a hard worker, always striving to get better, and I'm not surprised that he figured it out quicker than I thought he would. That's the kind of athlete he is.

"Baseball is Troy Tulowitzki's life. He loves the game and he plays it the way it should be played."

The only thing Tulowitzki wears more than his passion is his allegiance to the Dirtbags. Years removed, he still wears Dirtbag t-shirts under his uniform, and his parents wear Dirtbag apparel more often than they do Rockie gear.

Tulowitzki is the Dirtbags' "natural," and it all comes quite natural for him.

Comparisons are odious, or so the phrase goes when it was born six centuries ago and used often by writers of great reputation and wit. It doesn't mean they stink; it means they are offensive.

They can be telling, though, in examining how effective a modern player has been when contrasted to a Hall of Famer, which is what we're doing here with Dodger legend Sandy Koufax and Angels star and former Dirtbag Jered Weaver.

Weaver began 2013 with a 102–53 record with an ERA of 3.25 in his first seven seasons. His personal win percentage is .658. His team's winning percentage in games he started is .622. He has had a quality start in 67 percent of his starts through 2012, and Weaver left a game poised to collect a win seventeen other times, but the bullpen let it get away.

Jered Weaver is the only Long Beach State baseball player to win the Golden Spikes Award as player of the year, in 2004. *Courtesy Long Beach State.*

Weaver is one of seven active players to reach one hundred wins in his first seven seasons; he set a record as a rookie for consecutive wins (ten); in 2010, he had 233 strikeouts and twenty-seven quality starts in thirty-four outings, a year in which he was 13–12 record and the bullpen blew six potential wins; he opened 2011 6–0, the fourth pitcher all-time to win six games in April; threw a no-hitter in 2012; and went 20–5 in 2012.

Koufax had six seasons at the end of his career that are widely considered to be the best six in baseball history. He was

129–47 from 1961 to 1966 (.656 win percentage), 78 percent of his 211 starts were classified as quality starts (six innings or more, three earned runs or less); and his ERA during those six years was 2.20.

Koufax's six monstrous seasons will likely stand all tests of time, and that's not the point. It's just that Weaver's numbers indicate how effective he has been without a lot of public acclaim. Weaver finished a low-key second and third in Cy Young balloting the last two seasons.

Everyone who saw him pitch at Long Beach State knew he was destined for greatness. He was 37–8 in three seasons with a 2.43 ERA and 431 strikeouts in 370 innings. He had seven games with 14-plus strike outs and opened the game with 10 strikeouts twice in 2004, against USC and BYU.

Weaver rivals Tulowitzki in his born-to-be-a-Dirtbag devotion to the program. The younger brother of former Major Leaguer Jeff Weaver starred at Simi Valley High and was recruited hard by several schools, including Cal State–Fullerton, but his choice was easy.

"I couldn't pass up being a Dirtbag," he told the *Press-Telegram*'s Gordie Verrell in 2004.

And he had the team mentality that is the essence of the program. For all of his personal achievements, including being named college baseball's player of the year in 2004 and winning the Golden Spike Award, his emphasis was always on the team's record.

"I'm here for the team," he told Verrell. "I've always been a team guy. All I've ever been interested in is helping my team to the next step."

Besides his pitching, several things in his career have underscored that attitude. One is the way he handled his draft status with the Angels. Because his agent was Scott Boras, he fell to the twelfth pick in the first round over signability and financial issues. The Angels and Boras butted heads for months and cost Weaver a prompt start of his career before they finally came to terms.

He never held it against the club. "I realize this is a business, and business is business," he told the media after signing. "I'm not mad at anyone, and I don't hold any grudges. I love being with the Angels, and we have a terrific clubhouse with a bunch of good guys who are fun to be around. I love pitching here where a lot of my friends from Long Beach can come out and see me play."

Finally, there was his 2011 decision to sign a five-year, $85 million deal with the Angels and stay in his hometown rather than chase the free agency lottery.

"How much money do you possibly need?" Weaver said to reporters when asked why he agreed to stay in Los Angeles. "I've never liked the business side of all this. When I knew the Angels wanted to get this done, I told Scott [Boras] I wanted to stay in Southern California."

Weaver has become a team leader. He married his college sweetheart, former 49ers soccer player Kristin Travis; took a big crowd of family and friends to his induction into the Long Beach State Hall of Fame; and became the team spokesman and soul of the team during the Nick Adenhart tragedy.

Years removed from the car accident that cost Adenhart his life, Weaver still walks to the fence where Adenhart's number is displayed and gives it a tap before every game.

Chapter 11

THE REAL BOYS OF SUMMER

Twenty years later, Jeremy Hess is still airborne.

It was late August 1993 in Williamsport, Pennsylvania, home of the Little League World Series, and forty thousand rabid fans were enthralled as the twelve-year-old scamp came to the plate as a pinch-hitter for the Long Beach Little League team with the bases loaded, two outs, bottom of the seventh and the score tied 2–2 with Panama in the championship game.

On a 0–1 pitch, Hess drilled a single off the right field wall to drive home the game-winner and give Long Beach the 1993 title.

The picture seen on ABC and in hundreds of newspapers was Hess leaping down the first base line and then jumping into the arms of coach Jeff Burroughs after the winning hit, his own *Titanic* "I'm on top of the world!" moment. But truly, all of the images taken of the Long Beach team at Williamsport are indelible shots of young men having the time of their young lives.

The 1993 team won its second consecutive title. The 1992 team won the U.S. title before losing the title game to the Philippines team that would soon after forfeit the win because of ineligible players.

The '93 team is the one people remember because of the huzzah over a second appearance and the childlike glee the team, led by Sean Burroughs, Kevin Miller and Alex DeFazio, embraced and exhibited during its stay. It was Long Beach's first Little League title but, in actuality, an extension of a long history of successful Long Beach youth teams dating back to the beginning of American Legion play in the late '20s.

The hit that won it—Jeremy Hess came off the bench to single to right field to drive in the game-winning run in a 3–2 title game win.

The 1992–93 teams were a solid family of youngsters who had been playing sports together for years before getting tickets to Williamsport. Several players were teammates in AYSO leagues, would attend pool parties at each other's homes and go on group surfing trips.

"They went everywhere together," recalls Larry Lewis, the lawyer who was head coach of both teams. "They were one big family. They had remarkable chemistry. The kids genuinely liked each other. There was no divisiveness."

"The cool thing about that group is that we were always together," said Kevin Sullivan, a member of the 1992 team. "There were guys I played with from T-ball all the way to Williamsport. We had a chemistry that I'll never forget or ever have again."

"I think we all grew up in balanced homes," said Ryan Beaver. "We got along incredibly well. That has to be what people call team chemistry."

Team chemistry was often displayed as team fun. Their escapades would have neatly fit into the script for the seminal Little League film, *The Bad News Bears*.

Sean Burroughs, the son of Jeff Burroughs, threw a no-hitter during the 1993 Little League World Series.

Sean Burroughs enlivened both teams with his pounding of the plate with his bat to "summon the home run gods" and told a reporter that when he grew up he wanted to be a gynecologist. Players were guilty of so much tomfoolery at the Williamsport barracks that they were banned from the pool.

Charlie Hayes, Billy Gwinn and DeFazio commandeered a golf cart in Williamsport and drove it into a building. They took turns sliding down the steep hill behind the center field fence. Ali Strain-Bay and Randall Shelley were ringleaders of barracks foolishness.

One night, Jeff Burroughs, Sean's dad, Lewis's top assistant and the former Wilson star who was the American League 1974 MVP, went looking for Hayes in the barracks and found him sleeping in a trash can.

"We had a ridiculous time," said Hayes. "I'm surprised we got away with some of the things we did." An official at Williamsport gave the team a double-edged compliment when he said it was "the most unruly" team he'd ever seen off the field and "the most disciplined" team he'd ever seen on the field.

"We let them mess around and have fun," Lewis said. "They played the game because they liked it, not because someone made them. We always told them to have fun and show people what they could do."

Sean Burroughs said the biggest misconception is that the teams were hooked to a baseball IV. "People think we lived for baseball, but we didn't. A lot of us were beach rats who also played baseball. We'd play hard for six innings and then go surf. We were there for the baseball, but we were also there for the fun—food fights, pillow fights, whatever we could find," he said.

"It was the most fortunate thing that could happen to a kid, not just because we won but because it was fun," Beaver said. "We had the absolutely greatest time any group of kids could have. For all that the coaches did for us, it was just as important that they let us be kids."

All but two of the twenty-three players went on to college, ten played college baseball and Burroughs would be a first-round draft choice of the San Diego Padres and played nine years in the majors.

The 1992 team went 22–0 but never received the recognition it deserved because it never got to run the field in Williamsport with the championship banner. Beaver, who started the title game and endured a seven-run first inning, said the on-field loss served a life purpose.

"It helped me deal with failure and success," said Beaver. "They knocked me around for three innings but more people complimented me for what I did that day than anything else I did. They respected me for hanging in."

The 1993 team went 24–1 but had to win five games in five days after suffering a loss in divisional double elimination play and trailed 2–1 in the title game.

The 1992 team included Ryan Beaver, Sean Burroughs, Alex DeFazio, David Gonzalez, Michael Holden, Dane Mayfield, Chris Miller, Kevin Miller, Randall Shelley, Ali Strain-Bay, Ryan Stuart, Kevin Sullivan and Jeff Warshauer.

The 1993 team had Burroughs, DeFazio, the Millers, Billie Gwinn, Charlie Hayes, Jeremy Hess, Brent Kirkland, Timmy Lewis, Nate Moeiny, Travis Perkins, Scott Tobis, Cassidy Traub and Brady Werner.

There undoubtedly are plans for a twentieth-anniversary celebration of the 1993 title, and if someone commandeers a golf cart or takes a nap in a trash can, consider it just a second chance at a fantastic childhood.

Champions! The 1993 Long Beach Little League team carries its championship banner around the field after their title game win.

Long before the boys of summer circa 1992–93 took Williamsport, Long Beach was putting together national and state champions in other youth leagues, especially in the early days of American Legion play.

Long Beach post teams won department or state titles in 1930, 1937, 1944, 1945, 1963, 2010 and 2012. The 1963 team representing Peterson Post won a national title, and a Lakewood-based team won a regional title in 2012.

The 1963 team was unique because it essentially was the same Long Beach Poly team that won the CIF title under John Herbold. Fifty years later, the memories still resonate.

Herbold had three ace pitchers in Bob Wiswell, Jerry Flynn and Terry Roe; a future Major Leaguer in Oscar Brown, brother of Willie and Ollie;

and a relay team of base-running whippets in second-baseman Richard Dash and shortstop Ike McCraw. The Jackrabbits did not allow an earned run in their five playoff games.

Herbold said '63 catcher Bob Von Eps was the best he ever coached. He had a solid first baseman in Jerry Martin, who was sidelined late in the season from a gunshot wound in a hunting accident. Larry Lauriha was the third baseman, Merrill Smith played alongside Brown and Flynn in the outfield and Ed Clapp was the fourth pitcher on the deep staff. Pryor Bailey, Jim Smith, Ron Kasper, Bill Goldston, Harold Armstrong, Bruce Ellinoy and Randy Humphrey rounded out the roster.

Gale Taylor was head coach, and former Major Leaguer and St. Anthony star Lou Berberet shared coaching duties with Ewing Turner. Longtime Parks and Rec chief Ray McKinstry, who served American Legion baseball for forty-five years, was team manager. Herbold was never far away.

After winning the legion's Harbor League title, the Nineteenth District tourney title and the state tournament in Yountville, they advanced to the Western States Regional, which was held at Blair Field.

Roe struck out sixteen in a three-hit 9–3 win over Tucson. Wiswell struck out fourteen and took a no-hitter into the ninth in an 8–0 win over Greeley (Colorado). After a loss to Roswell, New Mexico, Roe threw a four-hitter in a 5–0 win over Las Vegas, and Wiswell came back to avenge the Roswell loss by striking out a stunning twenty-one in a 10–0 title game win before 3,197 at Blair.

In the national championship in Keene, New Hampshire, Roe beat the Somerville, Massachusetts team 4–2, with McCraw hitting a home run and Brown driving in a pair; Wiswell allowed five hits and drove in four runs in

Bob Lemon (center) played American Legion ball for the Long Beach 27 post in 1936 at the age of sixteen.

an 8–1 win against Omaha; and Roe and Clapp combined on a 12–3 win over previously unbeaten Memphis, with Dash collecting three hits, three RBIs and four runs.

Flynn's three-hitter against Evansville put Long Beach in the title game, where they beat Memphis for a second time, 5–4, behind a pair of double steals worth two runs and tenacious pitching by Wiswell and Roe.

Dash was named player of the year at the tourney, and Brown won the Sportsmanship Award. Peterson went 37–4 on the season, with three of the losses coming in league play against their prep neighbors in Lakewood and Compton. Of the core group, five players signed pro contracts—Brown, Flynn, Wiswell, McCraw and Von Eps—and Brown made it to the majors, hitting .244 in five seasons with the Braves.

There was plenty of success in local legion play before the '63 team won a title. Bob Hughes, a plumber by trade, was the manager/director of the team from 1930 to 1950, and his teams are revered in legion history for the number of professional players they featured.

The 1930 team that won a state and Western Sectional title featured two pitchers—Lee Stine and Jack Salveson—and infielder Donald Lang. The 1936 and 1937 teams included Vern Stephens, Cliff Mapes, Bobby Sturgeon, Jerry Gardner, Eddie Bockman and Chuck Stevens.

The 1944 and 1945 teams won back-to-back state titles led by pitchers Harry Minor and Vance Thurston, catcher Kenny White and Morley Bockman, Eddie's younger brother.

In Connie Mack ball (ages sixteen to eighteen), eight national titles have gone to area teams: the Long Beach Cardinals in 1967, 1973, 1975 and 2002; the Bellflower-Compton Giants in 1969; the Compton Giants in 1972; the Norwalk Cardinals in 1986; and the Southern California Renegades in 2012.

The 1967 team, coached by renowned scout Bob Harrison, lost its opening game in the national tourney and then rebounded to beat Portland in the title game, 6–2, behind Randy Moffitt, Bruce Ellingsen, Jay Horne, Jim George, Fred Long and Willie Norwood.

The 1969 team beat Nashville for the title, 3–0, led by Steve Staggs, Eric Raich and Charlie Bates (Cal State Los Angeles).

The 2012 squad, which went 42–5 en route to the title, featured pitcher Chris Castellanos, who was playing his senior season for Poly in 2013 and already had a scholarship commitment from Stanford.

The 1965 PONY national championship team shows off its banner and trophies.

PONY Long Beach teams (ages thirteen to fourteen) have won national titles in 1959, 1965, 2008 and 2012, as did a 2002 team from Norwalk and a 2003 squad from Lakewood.

Harrison and Buck Arnold were the coaches of the '59 and '65 teams, the latter featuring future Major Leaguers Jeff Burroughs and Craig Swan. Swan had two complete game wins in the tourney and threw a one-hitter in the title game.

The 2008 team featured a bevy of kids who became high school stars and have since moved on to college or the pros—Chase DeJong (Wilson), a second-round pick in the 2012 draft; Thomas Walker (Poly), who is playing at Oregon; and Wilson's Brett Harper, Solomen Williams and Ty Provencher. Down 2–1 in the seventh in the title game, Oliver Van Buskirk hit a two-run home run for the win.

The 2012 team went 20–0 in postseason play, beating Chinese Taipai 9–7 for the title behind Jack Williford, Spencer Steer (who had a three-run home run in the title game) and Will Semons.

One of the country's premiere events each summer doesn't require much traveling. You just drive to Blair Field and watch three hundred of the top prospects in the nation compete in the Area Code Games.

Getting in, though, is difficult. The event is tailored for the players, baseball scouts, college coaches and agents. No tickets are sold for the games, and it's kind of eerie to watch a ballgame at Blair without much cheering beyond the family and friends of some players.

Bob Williams, a Northern California real estate broker and baseball fan, launched the event in 1987. He designed it as an all-California event with players and teams identified by their area code. The first event was in Lodi, but it later relocated to Long Beach and has been at Blair Field since the '90s.

It has since broken that all-Cali alignment and become a pinnacle event in a young player's career. Major League Baseball approves of the event, the twelve teams are sponsored by Major League scouting teams and it is now a national attraction.

"When I started, I tried to see every kid personally before inviting them," Williams said. "As we got bigger, we relied on major league scouts and it turned into a showcase that now attracts as many agents as scouts.

"From the beginning, it was always free for the kids, unlike some other showcase events. We survive by charging the scouts and college coaches and agents."

Scouts pay upward of $100 each, and many teams will send as many as ten scouts to the event. College coaches also are charged a similar fee and agents even more.

"I like to say you can tell people by their clothes and shoes," Williams said. "The players have cleats. The college coaches wear team gear. The scouts are nondescript, but the stopwatches and radar guns give them away. The agents wear Gucci."

The roster of notable players who spent time at the ACG at Blair reads like a section of *The Baseball Encyclopedia*—Tori Hunter, Albert Pujols (then known as Jose), Ryan Howard, Ron Halladay, Josh Beckett. Nomar Garciaparra, Pat Burrell, David Wright, Andre Ethier, Troy Tulowitzki, Jered Weaver, Clayton Kershsaw, Bryce Harper and Mike Trout, just to name a few.

Chapter 12

A LEAGUE OF THEIR OWN

For many baseball players located on the West Coast, playing in the Major Leagues was often a choice.

The Pacific Coast League (PCL) was a vibrant league that began in 1903 and thrived up and down the coast until the Los Angeles Dodgers and San Francisco Giants changed minor league business forever when they left New York. Gone immediately were the Los Angeles Angels, Hollywood Stars and San Francisco Seals. Within years, so were PCL franchises in San Diego, Oakland and Seattle.

From 1946 to 1951, the PCL was considered a AAA league, and from 1952 to 1957 it was classified as "open"—about as close as any minor league got to be considered by some as Major League. And that was more than enough for a lot of players who had brief Major League careers but became stars in the PCL—most notably, Jack Graham, Jack Salveson and Chuck Stevens.

Graham was a six foot three, power-hitting left-handed hitter at Wilson who signed upon graduation and was playing in the minors by the time he was nineteen. He had signed with the Yankees, which was certainly intoxicating, but it meant he was playing far, far behind Lou Gehrig.

Graham hit twenty-eight, thirty-six, twenty-nine and twenty-one home runs in his first four minor league seasons, but the Yankees never gave consideration to moving him up the farm system. In 1940, he was traded to Brooklyn, where power-hitting left-hander Dolph Camilli was at first. Graham kept hammering away, hitting thirty-one home runs with 107 RBIs

Jack Graham (Wilson) hit forty-eight home runs for the PCL's San Diego Padres in 1948. He was feted, along with his parents, by Long Beach mayor Burton Chase (middle) before a game.

in 1941 and twenty-five in 1942. A year later, he was called up—by Uncle Sam to serve in the war effort.

By the time he returned to baseball, he was twenty-nine. He started the 1946 season with the Dodgers, played two games and was sold to the New York Giants, where he hit fourteen home runs in one hundred games. He was sent to Jersey City in 1947, where he pounded thirty-four home runs with 121 RBIs, but the Giants at the time had Johnny Mize at first. At the end of the season, he was sold to San Diego in the PCL.

His 1948 season was terrific—he hit forty-eight home runs with 136 RBIs. It could have been even greater; he was on pace to break the PCL record for home runs in a season (sixty) when he was beaned by Red Adams.

"I was in a zone during that season," Graham said. "I had 46 home runs in late July, and I thought with two months left I had a good chance to break Tony Lazzeri's record. But I lost a fastball that came out of the shadows one

Sunday afternoon at Wrigley Field when we were playing the Los Angeles Angels, and the ball hit me in the head.

"I was sidelined until the final week of the season,'" Graham told Doug Krikorian in a 2002 *Press-Telegram* column. "I sometimes wonder how many homers I would have hit had I not been sidelined. But those are the breaks. I just feel blessed I recovered completely from the injury."

He missed forty-six games. Local icon John Herbold said he believed Graham would have hit seventy home runs if he hadn't been beaned.

That campaign earned him a return ticket to the majors, with the St. Louis Browns, where he hit 24 home runs and drove in 79. But by then he was thirty-three. He returned to the PCL for three more seasons—and 85 more home runs—before calling it a career. Graham hit 384 career home runs in the minors.

"Jack never liked much attention," Harry Minor said. "He always preferred to stay in the background. He could have chased the majors for a little longer. Even after that 1948 season, he wasn't sure he wanted to leave. The money in the PCL was better than some major league teams."

Graham remained involved in baseball locally after retiring. He was the manager of the Long Beach Rockets semi-pro team as well as an American Legion team. He worked as athletic equipment manager for twenty-five years at Lakewood and Wilson High Schools, worked the Blair Field scoreboard for summer youth games and helped scouts with their winter teams.

He was generous to a fault, too, buying his players gloves and equipment and helping raise money for local high school baseball programs.

"He'd do anything for the kids," his longtime friend Red Meairs told Gordie Verrell in a 1999 *Press-Telegram* article. "He was tough, but he'd give you the shirt off his back. When a kid needed a glove, or anything, he'd send him to the sporting goods store and tell him, 'Bring the bill to me.' That was the way he was."

It is a conceit of Major League fans to assume that a career isn't truly meaningful unless someone spent their careers at the top. That's a good way to miss meeting and knowing some truly admirable and accomplished athletes.

In the case of Jack Salveson, his brief five-year career in Major League baseball was perhaps the least exciting years he spent in sports.

Salveson was among the large group of locals in the '30s who made it to the majors. When he broke into the majors in 1933, he was the youngest player in the game. He played three seasons, for the Giants, Pirates and White Sox, from 1933 to 1935, going 4–6 in fifty-two appearances.

Rather than try to catch on with another team, he returned to the coast and the PCL.

In 1936, he pitched for the Los Angeles Angels and won twenty-one games with a 2.76 ERA. He played in L.A. two more seasons before going to the Oakland Oaks, where he played for four years and racked up almost three hundred innings per season. In 1942, he won twenty-four for the Oaks with a 2.58 ERA.

With many players serving in World War II, he was obtained by Cleveland for 1943 and had a stellar if brief season, pitching in twenty-three games with eleven starts, four complete games, three shutouts and three saves with a 5–3 record. He played for the Indians again in 1945, making nineteen appearances.

And then it was back to the PCL, for eight more seasons. He was 41–21 in a three-year period with the Hollywood Stars, helping them to the 1948 PCL title, and called it a career after 1953 with 204 wins in the PCL and 224 overall.

He was considered one of the truly nicest men in baseball. He was close with *Press-Telegram* sports editor Frank Blair and sent Blair a signed photograph thanking him for his support and friendship. He wasn't everyone's friend, however. Concession personnel at ballparks disliked him because he worked fast. PCL immortal Lefty O'Doul tagged Salveson as "The Great Conservationist."

"He was a delightful person and also a great guy to have on your club," said Chuck Stevens. "If Jack threw more than 100 pitches, it was a

Jack Salveson broke in with the New York Giants in 1933 for three years, then had a long minor league career in the Pacific Coast League before a return to the majors during World War II. He spent fifteen years in the PCL, playing for six different teams and winning 204 games. This portrait is signed by Salveson to former *Press-Telegram* sports editor Frank Blair, who helped push the city to build its own ballpark, which was posthumously named after the newspaperman.

devastating night for him. He pitched quick and everything was for a strike. He often pitched complete games in an hour and fifteen minutes, or an hour and twenty."

Salveson threw a hard sinker and induced ground balls, and as a result, his outings were prolific though brief. Stevens recalled the Stars' concession man, Danny Goodman (who went on to be the concession chief with the Dodgers), getting angry at the pace of Jack's games. "Danny ordered the infield to be dragged after the fifth inning of games Jack started so he could sell more hot dogs," he said.

The affable Salveson had a simple credo: "I'm going to throw just so many pitches. and they're going to hit me or not." As he showed, it was more often not.

Salveson had his share of unique Major League memories. As a preteen, he was a batboy for a pair of barnstorming games matching teams coached by Babe Ruth and Walter Johnson. After his one season at Long Beach City College, he was the last player signed by Hall of Fame New York Giants manager John McGraw.

He appeared in the *Pride of the Yankees* film featuring Gary Cooper as Yankee great Lou Gehrig. Salveson played the pitcher who beaned Gehrig. Using a sewn-up baseball with straw inside instead of cork, it took the brisk Salveson an onerous seven pitches before he finally was able to plunk Cooper.

The only person who can speak with more authority on Long Beach baseball than Harry Minor is Chuck Stevens, the Poly kid and St. Louis Browns first baseman who is ninety-four years old as of April 2013 and still involved with baseball as a resource for the Association of Professional Ball Players of America (APBPA), the organization he served as secretary-treasurer from 1960 to 1998.

Stevens had his trial with the Major Leagues. He signed with the St. Louis Browns after graduating from Poly and spent five years in the minors, hitting .290 with Toledo in 1941 to earn a late-season call-up with the Browns for four games.

He returned to Toledo in 1942 and spent three years in the United States Army Air Force serving his country. When he got out, he became the Browns' starting first baseman in 1946, playing in 122 games and hitting .248. He knew his days with the Browns were numbered; he spent 1947 back in Toledo. He started 1948 in St. Louis, hitting .261 in 85 games. He stayed with the Browns long enough to become the first player to get a hit off Satchel Paige in his Major League debut.

The Browns tried to option him out to the minors again, but he refused to report and packed up his family and headed home. A few weeks later, the Browns agreed to sell his contract to Hollywood.

He was just thirty but as happy as a ten-year-old. His parents took him to PCL games when he was eight, and he was as fascinated with them as a Yankee fan might have been fascinated by Babe Ruth. In the '20s and '30s, local newspapers covered the PCL, and Major League Baseball seemed distant.

"When I was growing up, the reputation of the major league didn't mean all that much," Stevens said in Carlos Bauer's fine book, *The Pacific Coast League: A Statistical Record, 1903–1957*. "The majors were far away, and so we cared much more about the Coast League.

"I especially remember that great 1934 Angel club with Frank Demaree, Jigger Statz, and Jimmie Reese. I was a fan of the Angels and the Stars. In 1933, the Stars held their training camp at Shell Field, and I would go watch them practice. I was there the day of that horrendous earthquake."

He spent six years as the regular first baseman for the Stars, playing sterling defense and hitting leadoff most years, usually around .300. The Stars won three PCL titles with Stevens, in 1949, 1952 and 1953.

"When I joined the PCL, I thought I had died and gone to heaven," he said in Bauer's book. "I was so glad to get away from that very bad club we had in St. Louis, and its even worse management. With the Hollywood Stars, I got a two-year contract that paid me more than I made in the majors."

The PCL's best teams drew well, the seasons lasted longer because of the climate, and team ownership treated the players well. Stevens said all of the PCL teams flew for long road trips; he had never seen the inside of a plane in his three Major League seasons. Stevens estimates that about 70 percent of PCL players were there by choice—they were closer to home, or paid better or just happy to be away from the capricious nature of Major League Baseball management.

Plus, you could play in shorts in the PCL. In 1950, the Stars introduced unique new uniforms—shorts and a thin t-shirt. It was unconventional but practical, considering the climate. It also served as a great publicity stunt. Stevens had the privilege of being the first player to hit in the shorts.

"It was the brain child of [manager] Fred Haney," Stevens said. "The shorts were tailored with sliding pads in the hips and we'd roll our socks up the knee. We filled every park in the PCL wearing those things," he told author Dick Dobbins in his 2001 book *The Grand Minor League*.

Stevens, who had small roles in two baseball films—*The Stratton Story* in 1949, starring Jimmy Stewart, and *The Winning Team* in 1952, with Doris

Day and Ronald Reagan—played through the 1957 season, as a playing-manager in 1956 with Amarillo, which won the league, before calling it quits. But he was by no means done with baseball.

In 1960, he was asked to become secretary-treasurer of the Association of Professional Ball Players of America (APBPA), a support group for former players in need of financial or medical assistance. Major League Baseball provided little in the way of pensions or health insurance for former players. When the reserve clause was broken and free agency opened the door to changes in this system, baseball set artificial barriers for coverage that eliminated several generations of prewar players.

Stevens modernized the group's bylaws to conform to tax laws, took advantage of alternate funding for coverage and handled the day-to-day contact with former players. He used whatever avenue he could to make sure former players and employees were aware of their services.

It was Stevens who came up with the idea, and sponsorship, for the Cracker Jack All-Star Game that was held at RFK Stadium in Washington, D.C., in 1982. It was a different kind of old-timers game; the veterans played their storied positions and played to win. He got most of the living Hall of Famers to attend or play, and the inaugural game featured Luke Appling, seventy-five, hitting a home run off Warren Spahn.

The game continued for several years with proceeds benefiting the ABPBA. Major League Baseball eventually stepped up and participated in the group.

"There were many players from my era and before that who were too proud to admit they needed help," he said, "or reluctant to seek it. The group made it possible for so many former baseball people to live with dignity."

He retired when he turned eighty but remains in contact with the organization and still serves as a conduit to multiple generations of ballplayers, major or minor.

Chapter 13

PROS AND CONS

There's nothing amateur about Long Beach baseball, with almost three hundred players with ties to the area having reached the Major Leagues. But the city has never had much success when it comes to having a pro team of its own.

That has proven to be an asset in many ways, putting the spotlight on youth baseball, ranging from the 1992 and 1993 Long Beach Little League World Championship teams, the long line of championships won by area high schools and the way Long Beach State has become a feeder school for the pros.

Baseball may be a summer game, but some of the bigger pro events in town staged here have actually taken place in the fall and winter.

The first "pro" team in Long Beach was the Long Beach Clothiers in 1910, playing in the well-named Southern California Trolley League since the six teams used the trolley system in Southern California to travel to games.

The Clothiers, owned and managed by S.J. Abrams according to *Baseball-Reference.com,* opened play in April along with the L.A. Maiers, L.A. McCormicks, Pasadena Silk Sox, Redondo Beach Sand Dabs and Santa Ana Walnut Growers. Obviously, most of the teams were owned or sponsored by local businesses.

And business closed early. The Maiers and Silk Sox folded on May 3, and the entire league disbanded on June 12.

Three years later, the Long Beach Beachcombers were part of the inaugural Southern California League. The Beachcombers went 43–46 before the league was disbanded on July 23. The San Diego Bears (56–33) and San Bernardino Kittens (48–38) finished ahead of them. The last place team began the season as the Pasadena Millionaires before a franchise shift to become the Santa Barbara Barbareans.

Two Beachcombers would make brief Major League appearances: pitcher Herb Hall, who was 15–11 for the Beachcombers, pitched in three games for the Detroit Tigers in 1918 and spent fourteen years in the minors, winning 230 games; and infielder Ray Grimes, who was just nineteen in 1913 and in 1920 would hit .158 in 20 games for the New York Giants. He had a nineteen-year minor league career.

The city got its first taste of real Major League baseball in 1918. On March 25, the Chicago Cubs played an exhibition game against Long Beach Poly, the Cubs taking a 4–1 win and future Hall of Famer Grover Cleveland Alexander pitching two innings of relief.

The opening of Shell Oil Park in 1922—on the corner of Stearns and Redondo—and Recreation Park in 1924 led to consistent appearances by Major League and Pacific Coast League teams in town, mostly for spring training games, barnstorming appearances or the California Winter League. Bill Feistner, the local promoter of all things sports, provided the idea for the Shell Oil team and served as its booking agent for games and acquiring players.

Shell Park's official dedication was on August 19, 1923, although games were played there earlier with parked cars of fans providing the left- and right-field lines, the depth of the outfield and occasionally lights when games went late.

On March 23, 1926, the reigning World Champion Pirates, with Paul Waner, Johnny Rawlings and Max Carey, played a spring training game against the Oilers at Shell Park, the Pirates winning 5–3. The Philadelphia A's of 1929 and 1930—including Jimmie Foxx, Al Simmons and Lefty Grove—used Shell as their spring training facility.

The California Winter League was an off-season collection of teams and barnstormers who filled their rosters with major and minor league players, including a team made up of Negro League stars, the Los Angeles White Sox, four decades before Jackie Robinson broke the color barrier in 1947.

A Long Beach team played one recorded game in 1913–14 and seven games in 1924–25, providing opponents for the White Sox, the White Kings (Pacific Coast League players) and Joe Pirrone All-Stars (Major Leaguers, including Babe Herman).

The Shell Oilers officially joined the league in 1925–26, going 2–9–1. In 1926–27, they went 26–11–1 and met the Philadelphia Royal Giants in a five-game championship playoff series. The teams split the first four games, and the fifth was never played.

Shell's team in 1928–29 met the Cleveland Giants (30–13–2) in the championship, the Giants winning in four games. William F. McNeil's book *The California Winter League* quoted the *Chicago Defender*: "Seven thousand, the largest crowd in the history of Shell Oil Park, viewed the ferocious attack of the mighty Giants" in a 10–5 win.

The black teams in the 1920s CWL were jammed with players who during their career never played in the majors but were later inducted into the Hall of Fame—Cool Papa Bell, Biz Mackey, Jose Mendez, Bullet Joe Rogan, Andy Cooper and Oscar Charleston.

The Shell team featured more than a dozen Major Leaguers and twice as many players who played in the PCL. The top names included Earl Averill (1928–29); George Blaeholder (1926–27); Johnny Kerr, Hal Rhyne, Ferdie Schupp, Smead Jolley and Hi Bell (with three seasons each); and Bill Sweeney (four).

The combination of the oil boom's receding and the Depression ended Shell's baseball team, although the park remained for several years, last used by the Hollywood Stars as a spring training facility in 1933 until the March 10 earthquake. The CWL lived on until the '40s.

Breaking the winter tradition somewhat, a summer brand of pro baseball arrived in the '30s. According to Bill Hillburg in a Feb. 21, 1993, *Press-Telegram* story, businessman Levi Howard sponsored a recreation league team featuring black baseball teams, and in the '30s, they went semipro and were playing in the Intercity league.

Fain's Colored Giants, the Studebaker Champions and Long Beach Giants were among the black teams in the league. Shell Refinery had a team in the league, and there were two Latino-based teams in Wilmington and Paramount, as well as the Nippon Giants, a Japanese American team that played out of Terminal Island.

The Long Beach Giants featured Earnest McBride, who would become a civic leader in Long Beach, and Poly football stars Walter and Lodusky McCowen, the first two African Americans to play football for the Jackrabbits.

World War II changed the landscape as baseball stopped being business as usual. Locally based teams made occasional California Winter League appearances after the Oilers. In the war-stripped season of 1942–43, Vern Stephens (Poly) and Long Beach transplant George Caster played for an All-Star team, and Jack Graham (Poly) and Cliff Dapper, the former Dodger and friend of Duke Snider, played for the Los Alamitos Naval Air Base Team.

Games featuring service teams were popular since they were often crammed with baseball talent. Red Ruffing, Harry Danning and Nanny Fernandez, who all moved to Long Beach later in their careers, played for the Service All-Stars in 1944–45, and another transplant, Irish Meusel, had a naval team led by Jack Rothrock.

Rec Park hosted several games, two of note. In 1945, the Service All-Stars opened the CWL season against the Kansas City Royals at Rec Park, which featured a young infielder from Pasadena who was reportedly headed to the Major Leagues.

Jackie Robinson started at shortstop and hit an inside-the-park home run in a 4–2 win. The *Pittsburgh Courier* wrote, "Paced by the peerless all-around play of Robinson, the Royals opened with a 4–2 win at Recreation Park. An overflow crowd attended. Robinson hit an inside the park home run and was riot on the base paths and fielded brilliantly."

A year later, Bob Feller's Major League All-Stars squad, which had a young outfielder/pitcher named Bob Lemon on the squad, faced a Major-Minor All-Star team filled by Long Beach stars, like Chuck Stevens, Eddie Bockman, Don Lang and Jack Graham.

Graham homered off Feller in that game before 3,500 fans to give the Long Beachers a 1–0 lead, but Lemon hit a two-run home run in the eighth to give Feller's team the win.

Lee Stine was a Poly grad who spent four years in the majors (1934–36, 1938), with his best season being 1936, when he appeared in forty games with the Reds and went 3–8. He finished his career in the PCL.

Besides Graham, Stevens, Lang and Bockman, other locals who played in the CWL included Ralph Buxton, Kit Carson, Cliff Mapes, Jack Salveson, Lee Stine, Bobby Sturgeon and George Stovall. One other player was Lou Novikoff, the "Mad Russian" who had a five-year Major League career during World War II, was a PCL veteran and became a star softball player on the perennial national championship Long Beach Nitehawks.

Barnstorming slowly ended with the breaking of the racial

barrier in the majors and as Major League salaries increased. The last notable barnstorming game was a 1949 game between Lemon's all-stars and Satchel Paige's all-stars. The Long Beach Rockets, the eponymous locally produced winter team, endured into the '60s.

There was a brief moment in the '60s when the possibility of a Major League team moving to Long Beach emerged. When the Los Angeles Angels were born in 1961, they played their first season at aging Wrigley Field and then became tenants of the Los Angeles Dodgers and Dodger Stadium from 1962 to 1965.

Angels owner Gene Autry chafed at being the Dodgers' tenant, especially since the club was charging the Angels for half of all stadium operations. By 1964, he was ready to leave, and he started shopping for a new park.

The city that interested him most was Long Beach. The city had the land at three locations—on the water where the Pike Shopping area now sits, land in the center of the city near old defense facilities and at a former military base on the east side.

Autry met with Long Beach mayor Edwin Wade. Autry agreed to put up the money for the stadium, and the city would provide the land. In retrospect, the sticking point should never have been an issue: Wade and the city council wanted the team renamed the Long Beach Angels.

Rocky Bridges is given his 1961 Long Beach Century Club award as athlete of the year by Angels owner Gene Autry.

Autry wanted no part of that, and he immediately switched his attention to Anaheim, which had a plot of land buffeted by freeways on all sides—and no concern over the team's name.

Professional baseball did finally occupy Blair Field, but not until 1995, and it had a sketchy ten-year history most noteworthy for opening up the beer spigots at Blair. Notable player sightings were rare, and teams operated on the dime.

The independent Western Baseball League launched in 1995 with the Long Beach Barracuda. Former Wilson star and 1974 A.L. MVP Jeff

Burroughs was manager. Before the season was half-over, the owners split, the smaller group seized control and the team changed its name in midseason to the Riptide. Burroughs's team wound up winning the league title. Interest in the 1996 team waned amid reports of debts with the city and ownership rumors about moving, which the team did a season later.

The league came back to Long Beach in 2001 for three seasons. The Breakers, managed by former Dodger catcher Steve Yeager, won the 2001 league championship despite a 36–54 regular season record. Interest never had a peak, and the franchise folded in 2003.

The Golden Baseball League, with a central ownership by the league, launched in 2005 and included the Long Beach Armada. The Armada had well-known managers—Darrell Evans, Yeager again and Gary Templeton—but little else.

The Armada promised renovations of Blair Field to the city as part of its tenancy, but by the end in 2009, the league was behind on its debt and offered to pay off the city by giving it the team bus. That wasn't nearly as embarrassing as the 2006 signing of Jose Canseco while Major League Baseball was dealing with ramifications of the steroid era. The shameless marketing tactic blew up when Canseco hit .169.

In its last hurrah in 2009, the Armada featured two notable former Major Leaguers. Hideki Irabu, then forty years old, had once been a high-priced New York Yankee import from Japan. He signed with the Armada with the provision that he did not have to make road trips, would only attend those games he started at home and could leave the park after his work was done. He was 8–5 in his one season.

The flip side of Irabu was Jose Lima, one of the most congenial and energetic pitchers in baseball during his thirteen-year career. He was 16–8 in 1998 and 21–10 in 1999 for Houston and 13–5 with the 2004 L.A. Dodgers, leading the franchise to its first postseason win since 1988.

He was trying to revive his career with the Armada and did so with a big smile. He attended every game and signed autographs and took pictures until the last fan left. He still had the ability to pitch but no longer had the velocity for the majors. Aside from the managers with a pedigree and the opening of the taps, Lima, who passed away in 2010 from a heart attack, was the only lasting positive presence in the ten years of independent baseball.

Chapter 14

THE SCOUT

There are enough notable numbers, records and statistics in this book on Long Beach baseball to fulfill the dreams of any stathead, but the most incredible one is this:

Harry Minor has seen virtually every player mentioned in this book play baseball.

He probably missed George Stovall, the pseudo–Poly Jackrabbit who took a few at-bats in the nineteenth century, and Downey product Rube Ellis, whose Major League career came and went a century ago, but few others. Jack Rothrock, the first player from Long Beach to reach the majors? He played for Rothrock when he was a minor league manager. Bob Lemon? Minor was fifteen the first time he took the same field as the future Hall of Famer.

He turned eighty-five in 2012, which means he's been playing, managing, scouting, analyzing, enjoying and representing the sport for about seventy-five years. He grew up in the first productive era of Long Beach sports, that which sent Lemon, Vern Stephens and a half-dozen others to the majors. He played the sport professionally in the postwar era when it first opened its doors to black ballplayers and the sport itself grew larger and deeper and expanded to both coasts. He became a full-time scout in the '60s, which was when the second great expanse of players from greater Long Beach ascended to the majors.

He spent the next fifty years watching the game as a scout at the top end of the chain, from the perspective of looking for the next wunderkind to finding that hustling ballplayer who could perhaps reach the pros on work ethic and spirit.

Harry Minor was a star athlete at Wilson and a member of the 1943 "Jinxbusters" Bruins football team that led Wilson to its first-ever win over Poly. He has had an extraordinary sixty-five-year career in professional baseball, going from the ranks of a player to one of the top scouts in the game.

He spent a lot of five decades with his childhood friends who stayed in baseball themselves and returned to the city. How many people played with and against Lemon, the prep star outfielder; and barnstormed with Lemon, the All-Star pitcher; and worked with Lemon the Major League coach, scout and manager; and then dined with him long after his Indian and Yankee days were behind him?

Minor is just one of several dozen scouts from Long Beach who had a major impact in their field. The trio of Minor, Bob Harrison and Jerry Gardner stand out, because they were contemporaries and highly successful.

Harry Minor admittedly has had the greatest life. He looks back at his career with the same awe he had the day he was thrown onto the field of an American Legion game as a fourteen-year-old.

"I've enjoyed every part of it," Minor said at his home early in 2013, which is full of reminders of old friends and baseball greats he crossed paths with. "I loved playing the game. I think I played in every league there was except for the American and National.

"I loved being part of those eras here and being part of so much history in the '60s. I was fortunate to have a great wife who understood what the game and job as a scout was all about."

He has enough stories to fill his own series of books, but his story gets priority here.

He was a three-sport star at Wilson who was part of one of the most memorable football teams in Long Beach, the 1943 Bruin football team that won the school's first-ever game against legendary Poly. That unit is forever known as the "Jinxbusters."

He played American Legion ball for the Ellbees, which earned regional and state titles. He started his pro career in 1947 and made a grand tour of North America in the process—Riverside; Waco; Keokuk, Iowa; Buffalo; Savannah; Ottawa; Birmingham; Little Rock; Salinas; and Wellsville, New York, with a two-year pause for the Korean War.

He started as a pitcher going 6–10 in 1947 in Riverside. He moved to the outfield and hit twenty-four home runs in Keokuk in 1949. He played for former Chicago White Sox Hall of Fame catcher Ray Schalk—one of those not involved in the Black Sox scandal—in Buffalo in 1950. He became a catcher in 1953, and some of his teammates in the '50s included Art Ditmar, Luke Easter, Hector Lopez and Chuck Essegian, the former Dodger and teammate of John Herbold at Stanford. When he became a player-manager in 1958 for the Milwaukee Braves' Wellsville team, he had a young pitcher named Phil Niekro on his team.

He told Milwaukee management in 1959 that Niekro was a prospect, but no one was that interested in a nineteen-year-old knuckleball pitcher. Call it his first scouting coup. Niekro made the majors in 1964 and the Hall of Fame in 1967.

He moved into scouting full-time in 1961, except for one year as a minor league manager in 1969. His first job was with the Milwaukee Braves, and he spent that year as an area scout in Southern California, mostly hound-dogging Wilson star Bob Bailey.

"You would concentrate on maybe ten players, get as close to them as you could, and do a lot of background work," Minor said. "I grew up with Buck and his wife, and the families were close. I knew Bob when he was a baby."

Minor and the Braves offered the Bailey family a $135,000 contract—"unheard of in that day"—that was structured around an insurance annuity that would net Bailey more money over time. "I thought we had him," Minor said.

Buck Bailey was close to Minor, but he was also close with Pirates scouts. The Pirates offered $150,000 cash. He signed with the Pirates, who promised him a quick promotion. The Braves had a third baseman named Eddie Mathews in Bailey's way. "Bob was always a great hitter," Minor said. "It didn't help him that there was so much hype around his signing with the Pirates or that Forbes Field wasn't a place for power hitters."

In 1966, Minor was following a pitcher at USC, Tom Seaver, who had already turned down a contract when drafted by the Los Angeles Dodgers in 1965. Minor and the Braves continued to pursue him, drafting him in June 1966, and Minor was on hand when Seaver signed with the Braves.

Harry Minor was a pitcher with the Riverside Dons of the Sunset League in 1947 when he was just nineteen. Minor's first managing job in professional baseball was with the Wellesville Braves in the New York Penn League from 1958 to 1960. He had a career .574 winning percentage as a minor league manager.

The deal went sour immediately. Seaver was still technically at USC when the Trojans played two exhibition games, and while he didn't play, baseball commissioner William Eckert voided the contract. The NCAA then ruled Seaver ineligible at USC. Seaver's family threatened a lawsuit against baseball, and Eckert ruled that any team could match the Braves' offer *except* the Braves. Three teams stepped up, the New York Mets won a lottery drawing and baseball history was changed.

"I hated losing a guy to a stupid rules violation," Minor said. "I had no idea at the time he was going to become *Tom Seaver*, of course."

In 1968, he left the Braves to work for the New York Mets, starting a forty-year career with the organization. He worked as an area scout and then became a cross-checker, a scout who would travel the country to look at prospects on the recommendation of area scouts.

"At one time, I was the only cross-checker the Mets had," Minor said. "Someone had to see all of the top players firsthand. It was the only way you could put them in any kind of order.

"The travel was terrible. It would be a different town every day. Road maps, hotels and bad weather. It really wasn't scouting, because you were looking at players other scouts had picked. You were just preparing and comparing.

"But it was always satisfying to go to a town and see someone like a Dwight Gooden when he was in high school. I felt good when the Mets drafted Darryl Strawberry, because I had to fight for him. I gave a good report on a tiny, hard-working kid named Lenny Dykstra who went on to outperform a lot of first-round draft picks."

Minor's recommendations led to all three of those players being drafted and signed by the Mets and a part of the Mets' 1986 World Series championship team. His days with the Mets also led to a close friendship with Casey Stengel; Minor would occasionally serve as Stengel's chauffeur for speaking engagements.

He was hardly the only notable scout working out of Long Beach. In the '70s, almost two dozen scouts of all types lived in town. The trio that stood out were Minor, Bob Harrison and Jerry Gardner. Like Minor, Harrison and Gardner were homegrown graduates of Jordan High in 1938 who played ball together and entered scouting after their playing careers.

Harrison played semipro ball after high school, served in World War II and then returned to Long Beach as a welder at the Naval Shipyard and youth baseball coach. He was co-manager of the Long Beach team that won the PONY League national title in 1959; won a second PONY title in 1965 featuring Jeff Burroughs and Craig Swan; and in 1967 led a Connie Mack League team featuring future pros Randy Moffitt, Bruce Ellingson and Willie Norwood to a national title.

He was a scout for the Angels and Cardinals until being hired by Seattle in 1976 as a regional supervisor. It was Harrison who went to Cincinnati to take a look at a kid at Moeller High, the son of a Major Leaguer, named Ken Griffey.

Harrison insisted that Seattle owner George Argyros, who wanted to take Cal State–Fullerton pitcher Mike Harkey, take Griffey. "I'll never forget George saying, 'You better be right,'" Harrison said. He was right often. More than twenty-five Major Leaguers were drafted and signed on his recommendation.

Gardner was a prep catcher who attended a tryout camp in Riverside in 1939. "You can trace my entire career in baseball to that tryout camp," he said. "It lasted three days because of rain, but at the end I was signed by the St. Louis Cardinals. That would change my life forever."

He played in the Cardinals system until entering World War II in 1943. He returned to pro ball in 1947 and spent nine seasons in the minors as a player

Jerry Gardner was one of the top scouts in the Long Beach area for three decades.

and manager before taking a scouting job with Pittsburgh that lasted for thirty-five years and included the scouting and signing of the likes of Bob Bailey and Barry Bonds. He briefly worked for Atlanta and Tampa.

Minor eventually became a Major League scout for the Mets, helping the team assess Major League players they were pursuing via trades or free agency. It's what he was doing when he finally decided to retire in 2008.

"I had no secret formula, other than never missing a game," he said. "The more games you see, the more you know. Everything reminds you of someone you've seen in the thousands of players you've scouted. Experience makes you better.

"Anytime I have the opportunity to be around baseball people and baseball fans, I never pass it up. Baseball is such a great game, and it gave me such a great life."

Chapter 15

THE BABE IN LONG BEACH

There weren't many places that Babe Ruth didn't visit during his illustrious career and life. But only a few can say he was arrested in their city.

The New York Yankees outfielder was well on his way to legendary status when he scheduled a visit to Long Beach on January 22, 1927. He had won eighty-nine games as a pitcher in five and a half seasons with the Red Sox, had been the major figure in one of the most outlandish trades in baseball history and, by the age of twenty-six, had already set the Major League career record for home runs.

He was on an appearance and barnstorming tour when he came to Long Beach to play in an exhibition game and put on three shows at the State Theatre, which was located on the ground floor of the Jerkins Trust Building on Ocean Boulevard.

As appearances go, it was pretty much dog-and-pony. Ruth would get on stage, talk about baseball and give tips on fielding and hitting to a rabid audience of kids. At the end of the program, he'd give away signed baseballs. His schedule usually included a stop at a business or two where he would dine or be feted by local merchants.

Before his first show, theater manager Roy Reid came by his dressing room to warn Ruth that a warrant had been sent to the Long Beach Municipal Court that has been issued in San Diego.

The charge: a violation of child labor laws, by having kids appear on stage with him without a permit from the state labor commissioner.

Yankee icon Babe Ruth visited Long Beach several times, none more noteworthy than a January 1927 visit when he was fined for taking kids out of school to participate in a local appearance. He paid his $500 fine in person. *Courtesy Long Beach Public Library.*

As dutiful as an umpire calling a strike, Long Beach deputy commissioner Harvey Fremming arrived at the theater, informed Ruth of the warrant and made the arrest.

He was taken to the downtown police station, formally charged and informed of the fine. After some initial griping about the sanity of the situation, Ruth grinned and took out a wallet and counted out "25 crisp

$20 bills," according to the *Press-Telegram*, and handed them to desk sergeant Joe Hale.

"They forget how much I've done for kids," Ruth said to reporters leaving the station. "I've done nothing that would harm them. I've only tried to give them a little sunshine."

Ruth then was accompanied back to the theater by police officers, including Deputy Commissioner Fremming, and resumed his show, with Fremming saying he saw nothing in Ruth's show that was a violation of child labor laws.

The *Press-Telegram* went into attack mode on the outlandish nature of the charge. "Ruth's arrest illustrates how a man's love for children sometimes acts as a boomerang. His chief motive in getting the boys on the stage and presenting them autographed baseballs was to give pleasure to the boys themselves.

"In hundreds of American cities and in every village and inhabited part of the United States where there are boys there will be found a worshiper at the shrine of Babe Ruth. The redoubtable King of Swat has perhaps given more pleasure to boys than any one living man."

Ruth's trip west wasn't done. Rain scrubbed the exhibition game, but local car dealer Glenn E. Thomas, of the Long Beach Auto Company now known as the eponymous Thomas Dodge, had invited Ruth and one of his teammates, a fellow named Lou Gehrig, to go hunting at what was then a wooded area east of downtown that today is best known as the protected wetlands area.

Thomas took pictures of the day's activities, including a shot of Ruth, Gehrig and Thomas holding some freshly shot ducks and a long, wide-lens photo of the two ballplayers and the various dealership personnel who were on the hunt, standing in front of some of Thomas's latest vehicles.

One of those pictures still hangs on the wall of the Glenn E. Thomas Dodge showroom.

Ruth promised to return for an exhibition game following the 1927 season. It was set for October 30 at Shell Park, and five thousand tickets were sold, but rain again intervened.

On his 1931 exhibition tour, Ruth finally played a game of baseball at Houghton Park. He played first base and hit two home runs in a 19–3 rout of the Shell Oilers. People who were there said it was an arresting performance.

Chapter 16

THE HIGH SCHOOLS

The Moore League was launched in 1958 and named after legendary Long Beach Unified Sports director Harry J. Moore, making it one of the few leagues in the CIF-Southern Section leagues named after a local official.

The league has always included Poly, Wilson, Jordan, Lakewood and Millikan. Downey and El Rancho once were members, and Compton has been a member since early in the league's history. Cabrillo was opened in 1996.

The other two schools included here are St. Anthony's, which is located in downtown Long Beach, and St. John Bosco, the other prominent Catholic school, which is on the border of Long Beach, Lakewood and Bellflower.

The desire to include other schools that have been historically covered by the *Long Beach Press-Telegram* was a victim of space, but a list of Major League players from Gahr, Norwalk, Downey and other schools are listed in the registry.

Poly opened in 1895 as Long Beach High School and eventually was renamed Long Beach Poly. It was named *Sports Illustrated*'s School of the Century for its athletic excellence.

CIF-Southern Section Championships: Four, two official, two unofficial.

1912–1913: Poly went 17–5 in 1912, an era before there was postseason play. CalHiSports.com, the recognized authority on prep sports in California, named the '12 team its state team of the year retroactively. Technically, it's not a championship, but it does reflect the strength of Poly's history. A year later, Poly went 19–3–1, and CalHi past-posted the Rabbits as their state team of the year.

1936: Led by coach Lyle Kinnear, Poly won its first official CIF title, 14–4, over Escondido at Burcham Field behind the play of first baseman Chuck Stevens, third baseman Bob Gourbould, second baseman Vern Stephens, shortstop Bobby Sturgeon, outfielder Dick Lang and pitcher Joe Skeber. Nine Jackrabbits from the '36 team played professionally. Poly beat Montebello 11–1 and Paso Robles 5–2 on the way to the crown.

1963: John Herbold coached Poly (21–4) to its first title in more than a quarter-century with an amazing performance by pitchers Bob Wiswell and Terry Roe, who didn't allow a single earned run in the five playoff games. Wiswell (nine wins on the season) threw a one-hitter in the opening win over Santa Maria, 6–1. Roe relieved in the second game, a 3–1 win over Mayfair, and Herbold rode Roe the next three games—a one-hitter against Hawthorne (11–2), two-hitter against Lynwood (1–0) and three-hitter in the title win over Western (4–0) at LaPalma Park. Catcher Bob Van Eps was sturdy, and future Major Leaguer Oscar Brown and infielders Richard Dash and Ike McCraw ran teams to exhaustion. Virtually the same team also won the American Legion title that summer.

Joe Duhem was one of the finer players to come out of Poly who never reached the majors, spending eight seasons in the minors, including two with the Hollywood Stars.

Frank "Dink" Gabler had one great major league season, going 9–8 with a 3.12 ERA in 1936 with the New York Giants. He continued to pitch in the minors into his early forties.

Other title game appearances: Three. 1914, 1942, 1968.

All CIF-SS (first team except where noted): 1935: 1B Chuck Stevens. 1936: P Joe Skebar, 3B Bob Gourbolud, Stevens, SS Bobby Sturgeon (2) 1937: 2B Vern Stephens (2). 1938: 3B Jim Burris, 1B Gene Pickett. 1940: 3B Leroy Koenig. 1941: 3B Don Shirey. 1942: 1B Keith Simon. 1943: 3B Lynn Stone. 1945: SS Rocky Bridges. 1960: OF Brian McCall, P-OF Tommie Sisk (3). 1963: OF Oscar Brown, SS Ike McCraw, P Terry Roe (2). 1966: 3B Steve Smith (1), P Randy Moffitt (3). 1968: 2B Jerry Jaso, P Jim George. 1970: SS George Ambrow. 1977: OF Tony Gwynn. 1982: OF Chris Gwynn. 1985: P Erick Bryant. 1997: 2B Chase Utley. 2002: P James McDonald. 2005: Nolan Routt. 2010: 1B Thomas Walker. 2012: P Chris Castellanos.

Player of the Year: Ambrow (1970).

Major Leaguers (Twenty-five): Jack Rothrock (1925–32, 1934–35, 1937, Jack Salveson (1933–35), Lee Stine (1934–38), Kit Carson (1934–35), Frank Gabler (1935–38), Ralph Buxton (1938, 1949), Don Lang (1938,

1942), Bob Sturgeon (1940–48), Vern Stephens (1941–55), Chuck Stevens (1941–48), Jack Brewer (1944–46), Rex Cecil (1944–45), Rocky Bridges (1951–61), Brian McCall (1962–63), Tommy Sisk (1962–70), Ollie Brown (1965–77), Oscar Brown (1969–73), Randy Moffitt (1972–83), Willie Norwood (1977–80), Tony Gwynn (1982–2001), Chris Gwynn (1987–96), Nikco Riesgo (1991), Milton Bradley (2000–2011), Chase Utley (2003–2013), James McDonald (2008–2013).

Also (Three): George Stovall (1904–1915), Zeb Terry (1916–1922), Lyn Lary (1929–1940). Poly was playing baseball before there were rules regarding high school eligibility. These three players had loose connections to Poly. Stovall played in three games for Poly at the age of twenty-two in 1899. Terry reportedly graduated from Poly in 1910 and Lary in 1925, but they transferred in late in their high school days and there are no records indicating they played at Poly.

Major League umpires (One): Charlie Williams.

Wilson opened in 1925 and is a California Distinguished School.

CIF-SS Championships: Four.

1940: Al Johnson coached the Bruins to their first CIF title. Wilson won its way to the finals and earned the title off the field when San Diego withdrew from the game, refusing to play at Wilson. It went down in the record book as a 9–0 win.

1947: Johnson gave the reins of the team to Cliff Meyer before the season, and Wilson, behind pitcher Vance Thurston (16–0), went 26–1 and ran away with the crowd with a 24–1 win over Fullerton, 7–2 versus S.D. Hoover and 2–1 for the title over Glendale on Wilson's home field.

1950: Meyer won his second title behind Bud Daley and Frank Followell, going 24–3. Daley (Colton, 4–2) and Followell (Santa Ana Valley, 3–0) had back-to-back playoff no-hitters, and Daley got the win in the 5–4 title game at Santa Barbara. Followell's 1949 season was something to behold, too, throwing four no-hitters, including back-to-back no-nos.

2007: A more than fifty-year drought that included several near-miss titles and a bevy of future Major Leaguers came to an end when Andy Hall's team went 32–3, beat Canyon 5–1 for the CIF title at Dodger Stadium and was then named *USA Today*'s national champion. Elliott Glynn earned player of the year honors, and Ryan Dent was the fulcrum of the lineup and defense.

Other title game appearances: Six. 1939, 1941, 1999, 2000, 2004, 2008.

All CIF-SS (first team except where noted): 1937: SS Bob Lemon. 1938: Lemon, 3B Eddie Bockman (3). 1939: C Clarence Evans, Oren

Vance Thurston (left) was one of the best high school stars at Wilson, where he was coached by Cliff Meyer (center) and won a 1947 CIF title.

Skeith. 1940: C Lyle Otis, 2B Red Meairs (2). 1941: OF-P Al Brightman, Meairs. 1942: OF Ed McKenzie, SS Ted Herder. 1943: SS Dick Cole. 1944: OF Dick Ottele, C Ken White (2). 1945: 2B Skip Rowland, OF Harry Minor (2). 1946: Minor (2). 1947: OF John McKeown, P Vance Thurston. 1948: C Bob Henderson, P Frank Followell (3). 1949: SS Gene Painter, Followell (1), C Vernon Highfield (2). 1950: OF-P Bud Daley, Highfield, Followell. 1951: 2B Jerry Jeglum. 1953: 1B Jay Cook. 1954: 1B Cook. 1955: C Jim Pagliaroni, P Gordon Seyfried (2). 1959: C-IF Bob Bailey (3). 1960: SS Bailey (2). 1961: 3B Bailey. 1967: SS Bobby Grich. 1969: OF Jeff Burroughs. 1977: C Ron Thurston. 1998: 3B Sean Burroughs. 1999: OF Jeremy Hess, IF Keith Miller, P Chris Miller (2). 2000: Joey Pace. 2004: Ryan Schlack. 2005: SS Ryan Dent. 2007: P Elliott Glynn, SS Dent, OF Aaron Hicks (2). 2008: Zach Wilson, OF Hicks. 2012: P Chase DeJong.

Lean left-hander Frank Followell helped lead Poly to the 1949 CIF title.

Players of the Year: Lemon (1938), Thurston (1947), Followell (1949), Daley (1950), Bailey (1961), J. Burroughs (1969), S. Burroughs (1998), Glynn (2007).

Major Leaguers (Seventeen): Bob Lemon (1946–58), Eddie Bockman (1946–49), Jack Graham (1946, 1949), Dick Cole (1951–57), Bud Daley (1955–64), Jim Pagliaroni (1955, 1960–69), Bob Bailey (1962–78), Gordon Seyfried (1963–64), Casey Cox (1966–73), Andy Messersmith (1968–79), Bobby Grich (1970–86), Jeff Burroughs (1970–85), Ed Crosby (1971–76), Steve Connelly (1998), Gabe Gonzalez (1998), Sean Burroughs (2002–2006, 2011–12), Aaron Hicks (2013).

Lakewood opened in 1957 and is a magnet school for math scholars.

CIF-Southern Section Championships: Five.

1962: In the fifth year of the school's existence, head coach Artie Boyd led the Lancers to their first title with a 9–0 win over Montebello at Cerritos College. Jim Parks (12–2, 2.07 ERA) was the ace supported by future pro Jim Strickland. The route in the title game was the antithesis to the Lancers' season—they won five games during the season in their last at-bat, including coming back from a 5–2 deficit to beat Millikan for the Moore League title and overhauling a 5–2 deficit in a CIF semifinal win against Pasadena (6–5). They beat Norwalk (3–2), Western (4–1) and Riverside (1–0) to get to the semis. As a team, the players hit under .200 but found ways to win.

1970: In his second season at Lakewood, former Poly coach John Herbold earned Lakewood a second title with a 5–4 win over Ventura at Anaheim Stadium. Tom Lederer was the staff ace (10–0, 1.53) supported by future Trojan four-time College World Series player Russ McQueen. In the title game, Lederer got out of a two-out, runners-on-second-and-third jam by picking the runner off second. Lederer and McQueen were stout with playoff wins over Pius X 1–0, Buena Park 7–1, North Torrance 6–1 and Covina 5–0 before the Ventura game.

Damion Easley had one of the longest careers of anyone to come out of Lakewood High and Long Beach City College. *Courtesy Los Angeles Angels.*

1976: After losing in the finals in 1974 and 1975, a very flush Lakewood team beat neighbor Jordan 5–3 for the crown at Anaheim Stadium. Stan Williams and Dan Gausepohl were the team leaders.

1987: Spud O'Neil won his first title with a taut nine-inning 1–0 win over Esperanza at Dodger Stadium. Mike McNary (12–3, 1.38), who had twenty-nine career wins for the Lancers, led the staff and was supported in the field by Matt Nuez and future Major Leaguers Damion Easley and Chris Gomez.

2006: Keith Chipman (12–1, 1.07) allowed just one run to Agoura in the title game, but the Lancers (25–5–1) entered the bottom of the seventh down

1–0. The first two batters reached, and David Ross's double down the right field line at Dodger stadium drove in both for the win. Catcher Travis D'Arnaud was the big bat all season.

Other title game appearances: Five. 1974, 1975, 1977, 1994, 2002.

All CIF-SS selections (first team unless noted): 1962: P Jim Parks. 1964: P Jim Strickland (2). 1970: 2B Kim Hannaford, P Tom Lederer, P Russ McQueen (2). 1971: OF Doug Matter. 1973: P Doug Slettvet. 1974: SS John Flannery, P Greg Herman, P Floyd Chiffer (2). 1976: OF Bill Simpson, IF Don Ruzek, U Stan Williams. 1977: P Andy Bisnar, P-C Mike Fitzgerald (3). 1978: Fitzgerald (2). 1982: OF Bob Liebzer.1983: P Larry Casian. 1986: P Mike McNary. 1987: McNary, OF Matt Nuez (3). 1988: Nuez. 1989: 3B Ricardo Gutierrez, SS Chris Gomez. 1990: P Chris Miller. 1991: P David Resser. 1994: P Luke Fitzpatrick. 1995: P Steve Immel. 1996: IF Scott Holzhauer, OF Jon Weber. 2000: 1B Mike Hofius. 2001: Chris Basaldiva. 2002: David Balandan, Jay Lopez. 2003: 1B Mike Carp, OF Aijay Davis (2). 2004: Carp, Davis. 2006: P Keith Chipman, C Chase D'Arnaud, Jonathan Johnson. 2007: D'Arnaud, Trevor Costin. 2008: Jon Keener, SS Matt Duffy (2). 2009: Duffy. 2010: OF Hunter Jones, P-1B Jeff Yamaguchi. 2011: P-OF Nick Torres, P Shane Watson. 2012: Watson, SS J.P. Crawford.

Players of the year: Parks (1962), Williams (1976), McNary (1987), Gutierrez (1989), Chipman (2006).

Rod Gaspar, shown pitching in a Mets jersey at a Long Beach State alumni game, was one of three future pros at Lakewood in the '60s. He played at Long Beach City College and with the 49ers before a pro career that included being a key player on the 1969 New York Mets team that shocked baseball by winning the World Series.

Major Leaguers (Thirteen): Dave Marshall (1967–73), Rod Gaspar (1969–71, 1974), Tony Muser (1969, 1971–78), Jim Strickland (1971–73, 1975), Bruce Ellingsen (1974), John Flannery (1977), Floyd Chiffer (1982–84), Mike Fitzgerald (1983–92), Craig Grebeck (1990–2001), Larry Casian (1990–98), Damien Easley (1992–2008), Chris Gomez (1993–2008), Mike Carp (2009–2013).

Robert Andrews Millikan High opened in 1956 and is a COMPASS school for high achievers with several other campus college prep programs. It has award-winning music programs.

CIF-Southern Section Championships: Five.

1967: Millikan, which opened in 1956, won its first CIF title under head coach Bob Myers (1956–69), 2–1 over Santa Ana Valley at Blair Field. Future Major Leaguer Craig Swan got the win in relief. The tough-pitching Rams allowed just four runs in their five playoff games.

Dante Powell was a Millikan standout and the CIF player of the year in 1991. He played at Cal State Fullerton before a brief four-year major league career.

1969: In Myers's final season, the Rams and future Angels pitcher Dave Frost beat Santa Fe 9–2, in the first CIF title game played at Dodger Stadium. The nucleus of the '69 team made up the Peterson Post American Legion team that won a national title.

1983: In the first of three titles won at Anaheim Stadium, the Rams beat Colton 6–5, giving coach Dan Peters his first title.

1991: Dante Powell and Brian Keller led the Rams to a 8–2 win over Edison in the finals in Anaheim.

1992: For the first time since Chaffey won three straight titles (1956–58), the Rams posted back-to-back crowns with a 5–4 win over

Diamond Bar at Anaheim Stadium. It was also the fifth title won in a season in which Millikan did not win the Moore League regular season title.

Other championship game appearances: Four. 1984, 1989, 1997, 2001.

All-CIF-SS selections (first team unless noted): 1959: 1B Gary Brown. 1964: OF Mike Mantsch. 1967: 2B Jim Seida, P Craig Swan (2). 1969: OF Dave Chorley, 3B Rich Bailey. 1973: OF Steve Fenolglio, SS Doug Stokke. 1983: C Steve Brodie. 1984: OF Frank Meza. 1985: C Brian Turang (3). 1986: OF Ralph Lakin. 1990: OF Aaron Seja. 1991: OF Dante Powell, P Greg Gregory. 1992: OF Scott Allen. 1993: P Tony Palazzolo. 1995: P Eric Ireland, C Jeremy Sickles (2). 1996: Sickles (2). 1997: P Ryan Beaver, 3B Matt Williams. 1998: Tim Coltery. 1999: Preston Griffin. 2000: Griffin. 2001: P Matt Anderson, OF Matt Beard. 2009: P Josh Frye (1), 1B Jonathan Singleton (2).

Player of the year: Powell (1991).

Major Leaguers (Seven): Syd O'Brien (1969–72), Craig Swan (1973–84), Dave Frost (1977–82), Brian Turang (1993–94), Dante Powell (1997–2001), Nick Bierbrodt (2001–03), Mike Gallo (2003–06).

Mike Gallo was a three-school star in Long Beach. He played at Millikan, Long Beach City College and Long Beach State, where he led the 1998 Dirtbags to the College World Series. *Courtesy Long Beach State.*

Cliff Mapes, the first major leaguer out of Jordan High, gets some finer points and a little double-talk from Yankees manager Casey Stengel.

David Starr Jordan High opened in 1933 and now has a second campus for college prep students that is called "Baby Jordan."

CIF Title game appearances: One. 1976.

All-CIF-SS selections (first team unless noted): 1938: C Jerry Gardner (2). 1944: OF Ken Mapes. 1955: OF Ron Fairly (3). 1956: Fairly. 1959: OF Jim Berryhill. 1960: OF Bill Gaynor. 1976: P Terry O'Toole. 1988: SS Ray Holbert. 1990: SS Aaron Holbert. 1992: IF Marcus McCain.

Player of the year: Fairly (1956).

Major Leaguers (Seven): Cliff Mapes (1948–52), Bill Wilson (1950–51), Ron Fairly (1958–78), Gail Hopkins (1968–74), Leon Hooten (1974), Ray Holbert (1994–2000), Aaron Holbert (1996).

Compton Unified High School opened in 1896, and the campus later included Compton College, turning it into a school for grades eleven and twelve and two underclass years of college. It became a standard high school when Compton College moved to a new location.

CIF-Southern Section titles: Two.

1953: Outfielder John Core led the Charles Doyle–coached Tartars to a 5–2 win over La Jolla in San Diego. They took down Oxnard, 16–2, and Santa Barbara, 9–3, on the way to the title.

1961: Ron Woods and Paul Schaal led the Tartars to a second title, this one under coach Ray Edgmon. Compton had three one-run wins on the way to the title against a powerful El Segundo team and won 8–6 in nine innings at USC's Bovard Field.

Other CIF title game appearances: Two. 1938, 1951.

All-CIF-SS selections (first team unless noted): 1941: 1B Wayne Austin. 1942: OF Louis Gill. 1943: OF Duke Snider (2). 1948: 3B Jim Moore. 1949: 1B Jim Marshall. 1951: OF Don McPherson, P Bennie Daniels (2). 1953: OF John Core. 1956: OF Bob Henrich. 1961: OF Ron Woods, 3B Paul Schaal (2).

Major Leaguers (Fourteen): Duke Snider (1947–64), Bennie Daniels (1957–65), Bobby Henrich (1957–59), Dave Skaugstad (1957), Jim Marshall (1958–62), Don Rowe (1963), Paul Schaal (1964–74), Bob Watkins (1969), Odell Jones (1975, 1977–79, 1981, 1983–84, 1986, 1988), Dick Davis (1977–82), Gary Ward (1979–90), Reggie Walton (1980–82), Bob Pate (1980–81), Carl Nichols (1986–91).

Lou Berberet had a seven-year major league career and began it with the New York Yankees, where he unfortunately had a rotund catcher named Yogi Berra ahead of him.

Cabrillo opened in 1996 and joined the Moore League several years later.

St. Anthony of Padua opened in 1920 as a girl's school and, in 1940, added a boy's school. They merged as one in 1968.

Before he exploded on the scene with the Chicago Cubs and had a stint with the Los Angeles Dodgers, Nomar Garciaparra already had a determined look as a star shortstop at St. John Bosco.

CIF title game appearances: One. 1995.

All-CIF selections: 1947: C Lou Berberet (2). 1958: C Walt Osgood. 1961: P Walt Peterson (2). 1962: C Dave Adlesh. 1966: SS Bob Plutte. 1990: P Eric Mooney. 1991: IF Dan Guti. 1997: Joe Perry. 1998: Chris Luyben. 2000: Luyben. 2009: P Jeff Curran. 2010: Curran.

Major Leaguers (Three): Joe Amalfitano (1954–67), Lou Berberet (1954–60), Dave Adlesh (1963–68).

St. John Bosco opened in 1940 as an elementary school and expanded to include high school in 1953.

All-CIF-SS selections (first team unless noted): 1976: U Don Carfino. 1979: P Bryan Duquette. 1989: IF Martin Meza. 1990: Meza. 1991: Brent Bell. 1995: OF Edmund Muth. 1997: P Bud Smith. 2000: Ruben Salazar.

Major Leaguers (Four): Dennis Lamp (1977–92), Nomar Garciaparra (1996–2009), Bud Smith (2001–02), Evan Longoria (2008–2013).

Chapter 17

THE COLLEGES

Long Beach State was born in 1949 and started athletic competition four years later. The baseball team began play in 1954 as a member of the CCAA, later joining the PCAA (to become the Big West) in 1970. From 1977 to 1984, the team transitioned to Division I and played in the Southern California Baseball Association before the Big West instituted league play in 1985.

The program was underfunded as a Division I team and had just one winning season from 1973 to 1988, winning fourteen, sixteen and fourteen games in 1986–88. In 1989, then athletic director Corey Johnson decided to properly provide a full budget and hired Dave Snow as the head coach. In his first year, Snow's team went 50–15, improving on the 1988 team by thirty-six wins and earning the school's first-ever berth in the College World Series (CWS). The team picked up the nickname "Dirtbags" during that season, and it stuck for good in 1993.

College World Series appearances: Four.

1989 (50–15): Snow's first team won its first eighteen games, eclipsing the win total of 1988, and went 50–15, still the best record in school history. It swept its regional to advance to the CWS. Admittedly awed by Omaha, they dropped their first two games. Don Barbara hit .366, and the Dirtbags rotation featured Kyle Abbott (fifteen wins, 2.72), Andrew Croghan (12–1) and Tom Urbani (9–5).

1991 (45–22): The Dirtbags returned to Omaha after outlasting Oklahoma State in the regionals and got their first win, beating Clemson 8–5, in between losses to Wichita State and Creighton. Jason Giambi hit .407, Brent Cookson

Jered Weaver plays peek-a-boo during a windup at Blair Field. *Courtesy Long Beach State.*

had fifteen home runs and DH Scott Talanoa had eighty RBIs. Steve Trachsel (2.78) and Steve Whitaker (2.83) each won eleven games.

1993 (46–19): The Jeff Liefer–led Snowmen made their third CWS appearance in five years and came three outs away from playing for the title. After an opening loss to LSU, the Dirtbags beat Kansas and Texas A&M to earn a rematch with LSU, winning 10–8. They played LSU again for a berth in the title game and led 5–3 going into the ninth before LSU rallied for three to win. Daniel Choi set a school record with seventeen wins, and closer Gabe Gonzalez had thirteen saves and a 1.54 ERA.

1998 (43–23–1): After an opening loss to Miami, the Dirtbags eliminated Florida State and avenged the Miami loss with a 6–4 win. Arizona State eliminated the Dirtbags 14–4 the next day. The Gorilla Ball era lineup featured Chuck Lopez (.422), Paul Day (fifteen home runs, eighty-nine RBIs) and Terrmel Sledge. Mike Gallo and Jason Marr (nine saves) led the pitchers.

NCAA postseason appearances: Nineteen.

49er era: 1964, 1970.

Dirtbag era: 1989, 1991, 1992, 1993, 1994, 1995, 1996, 1997, 1998, 1999, 2001, 2002, 2003, 2004, 2005, 2007, 2008.

Conference titles: Eleven. CCAA (Two): 1964, 1969. PCAA (One): 1970. Big West (Eight): 1989, 1992–1994, 1996–97, 2003, 2008.

Troy Tulowitzki was a great defensive shortstop at Long Beach State and became even better when he made the majors with the Colorado Rockies. *Courtesy Long Beach State.*

All-Americans (first and second team, *Baseball America*, except for 1979): 1979, OF Rob Townley (1); 1989, P Kurt Abbott (1); 1990, 1B Don Barbara (1); 1991, P Steve Whitaker (1), P Steve Trachsel (2). 1993: P Daniel Choi (1). 1994, P Scott Rivette (2). 1995: 3B Jeff Liefer (2). 1998: 3B Paul Day (2). 2002: P Abe Alvarez (2). 2003: P Jered Weaver (1), P Abe Alvarez (2). 2004: Weaver (1); 2006: 3B Evan Longoria (2).

Other first-team All-Americans by other publications: 1991, DH Scott Talanoa; 1997, P Ara Petrosian; 1999: P Mike Gallo.

Player of the Year: Jered Weaver (2004).

Major Leaguers, 49er era (Six): Dick Nen (1963, 1965–68, 1970); Rod Gaspar (1969–71, 1974), Randy Moffitt (1972–83); George Throop (1975–79); Gary Beare (1976–77); Jim Smith (1982).

Major Leaguers, Dirtbag era (Thirty-seven): P Kyle Abbott (1991–92, 1995–96), OF Darrell Sherman (1993), P Steve Trachsel (1993–2008), SS Chris Gomez (1993–2008), P Tom Urbani (1993–96), OF Brent Cookson (1995, 1999), 1B Jason Giambi (1995–2013), P Gabe Gonzalez (1998), 1B/OF Jeff Liefer (1999–2006), P Marcus Jones (2000), P Rocky Biddle (2000–04), P Mike Gallo (2003–06), 2B Bobby Crosby (2003–10), P Chad Bentz (2004–05), P Abe Alvarez (2004–06), OF Terrmel Sledge (2004–07), OF Jeremy Reed

(2004–2011), 1B Paul McAnulty (2005–08, 2010), P Chris Demaria (2005–06), P Jason Vargas (2005–2013), P Jered Weaver (2006–2013), SS Troy Tulowitzki (2006–2013), P Carlos Muniz (2007–08), OF John Bowker (2008–11), 3B Evan Longoria (2008–2013), P Marco Estrada (2008–2013), P Andrew Carpenter (2008–2012), P Cesar Ramos (2009–2013), C Brad Davis (2010), P Bob Cramer (2010–11), P Vance Worley (2010–2013), 2B Danny Espinosa (2010–2013), P Jared Hughes (2011–2013), P Bryan Shaw (2011–2013), P Adam Wilk (2011–12), P Nick Vincent (2012), OF Shane Peterson (2013).

The first college in Long Beach opened in 1927, fielded its first athletic team in 1928 and promptly won a state title (in basketball). The state began regional and state playoffs for junior college baseball in 1950, and in 1954, the Vikings won their first of five and have reached the title series eight times, third-most in the state. The program has sent more than a dozen players to the Major Leagues, and twenty-six players and coaches have been inducted into the school's Hall of Champions.

State championships: Five.

1954: Joe Hicks won his first title as head coach as the Vikings beat Contra Costa. Roger Hull was the key bat in the lineup, and pitcher Jim Lee had fifteen wins and a school record 1.44 ERA.

1968: The Vikings beat Sacramento for Hicks's second crown, led by infielder Ed Crosby.

1969: Hicks and the Vikings made it back-to-back titles with a win over San Mateo.

1976: Bob Myers won a state title in his first season as head coach over L.A. Harbor College after serving as an assistant for six years and previously winning CIF titles at Millikan. Greg Harris was the star, going 18–4 on the mound and earning state player of the year honors, and Dan Gausepohl provided run support.

2006: Casey Crook coached the '06 Vikings to a 41–10 record and state title behind Tommy Peale, who was 16–0 with a 1.48 ERA and hit .341 with twenty-nine RBIs.

Other state title appearances: Three. 1953, 1963, 1972.

Major Leaguers (Fourteen): Jack Salveson (1933–35, 1943, 1945), Vern Stephens (1941–1955), Casey Cox (1966–73), Dave Marshall (1967–73), Rod Gaspar (1969–71, 1974), Syd O'Brien (1969–70, 1972), Ed Crosby (1970, 1972–73), Leon Hooten (1974), Dave Frost (1977–82), Craig Chamberlain (1979–80), Greg Harris (1981–95), Damion Easley (1992–2008), Brian Turang (1993–94), Mike Gallo (2003–06).

Chapter 18

THE LONG BEACH BASEBALL REGISTRY

A total of 134 players (and one umpire) reached the majors after playing at one of the seven Moore League schools (Cabrillo, Compton, Jordan, Lakewood, Millikan, Poly and Wilson), two Catholic schools (St. Anthony and St. John Bosco) and two colleges (Long Beach State, Long Beach City College).

Another eighty reached the majors playing for one of the many other high schools that have traditionally been considered part of "Greater Long Beach," which was defined by the *Long Beach Press-Telegram*'s circulation area that stretches as far west as Compton, east to Los Alamitos and north across the 5 Freeway to La Mirada. Included are Cal State–Dominguez Hills, Cerritos College and Compton College.

There are an additional 72 players who were born in greater Long Beach but didn't play at any of the local schools. That's 286 and doesn't include a number of players who lived and were involved in Long Beach sports but didn't play or grow up in the area.

Notes on affiliations: St. Louis refers to the Cardinals unless specifically noted as the St. Louis Browns; Philadelphia to the Phillies unless noted as the A's; Boston to the Red Sox unless noted as the Braves; Kansas City to the Royals unless noted as the A's; Milwaukee to the Brewers unless noted as the Braves; Washington to the Senators unless noted as the Nationals. All other multiple team cities are specific to the team (Mets, Yankees, Giants, etc.).

The attempt here has been as thorough as possible, but as always, there's a chance someone was missed or a CIF award was overlooked or unavailable. The author regrets any omissions.

Kyle Abbott / P / 6–4, 200
Born: February 18, 1965, Newburyport (MA).
High School: Mission Viejo.
College: University of California–San Diego, Long Beach State.
Drafted: 1989, first round, L.A. Angels.
Major League career: four seasons (L.A. Angels 1991, 1996; Philadelphia 1992, 1995).

Abbott was the first star pitcher of the Dirtbag era, winning fifteen games and posting a 2.73 ERA with 140 strikeouts. The saying that a pitcher has to be pretty good to have a 1–14 record is true. Abbott pitched well at times in 1992 despite that lopsided record for a Phillies team that won seventy games.

Dave Adlesh / C / 6–0, 187 / R-R
Born: July 15, 1943, Long Beach.
High School: St. Anthony's.
Major League career: six seasons (Houston 1963–68).

Adlesh made his debut at the age of nineteen in 1963 and was a backup catcher for the Astros in 106 games over six seasons. A highlight was catching the first of Don Wilson's no-hitters.

Abe Alvarez / P / 6–2, 190 / L-L
Born: October 17, 1982, Los Angeles.
High School: Fontana.
College: Long Beach State.
Drafted: 2003, second round, Boston.
Major League career: three seasons (Boston 2004–06).

Alvarez had a sterling career at Long Beach, going 23–5 with 195 strikeouts and a 2.56 ERA. His twenty-three wins is tied for fifth all-time, and he was the left-handed yin to Jered Weaver's right-handed yang for two seasons. His promising pro career was mishandled by Red Sox management. After nine minor league games, they promoted him to the majors for a start in 2003, and he was in the mix for a rotation spot for 2004 and 2005 but never got a full shot, making just three appearances in those two years.

Joey Amalfitano / 2B, manager / 5–11, 180 / R-R
Born: January 23, 1934, San Pedro.
High School: St. Anthony's.
College: Loyola Marymount, USC.

Major League career: ten seasons (N.Y. Giants 1954–55; San Francisco Giants 1960–61, 1963; Houston 1962, Chicago Cubs 1964–67). As manager: three seasons (Chicago Cubs, 1979–81).

Amalfitano is one of just a few players who played for both the New York and San Francisco Giants. He was a "bonus baby" in 1954 and had to be on the Giants roster for two years (twenty-nine total at-bats). He was a starter in four seasons, hitting .277 in 1960 and .271 in 1965 with the Cubs. He managed the Cubs for parts of three seasons (1979–81) and was a coach for most of his career, sixteen seasons as the third base coach for the L.A. Dodgers (1983–98).

Joey Amalfitano was a star infielder at St. Anthony's under head coach Hank Ennen. He had a ten-year major league career, most of it with the Giants, and then was a Dodgers coach for almost two decades.

BOB BAILEY / 3B / 6–0, 188 / R-R
Born: October 13, 1942, Long Beach.
High School: Wilson.
Major League career: seventeen seasons (Pittsburgh 1962–66, L.A. Dodgers 1967–68, Montreal 1969–75, Cincinnati 1976–77, Boston 1977–78).

See chapter eight.

GARY BEARE / P / 6–4, 205 / R-R
Born: August 22, 1952, San Diego.
High School: Kearny.
College: San Diego Mesa, Long Beach State.
Drafted: 1974, fifth round, Milwaukee.
Major League career: two seasons (Milwaukee 1973–74).

Beare led the 49ers in ERA in 1973 (3.44) and strikeouts in 1974 (eighty-two). His Major League trial was brief. He was 5–6 in twenty-three appearances in 1974.

CHAD BENTZ / P / 6–2, 215 / R-L
Born: May 5, 1980, Seward (AK).
High School: Douglas, Juneau (AK).
College: Long Beach State.
Drafted: 2001, seventh round, Montreal.
Major League career: two seasons (Montreal 2004, Florida 2005).

Bentz was born with a deformed right hand like Jim Abbott but served as a left-handed specialist for the Dirtbags. The Expos used him the same way in 2004, when he appeared in thirty-six games.

LOU BERBERET / C / 5–11, 212 / L-R
Born: November 20, 1929, Long Beach; Died: April 6, 2004.
High School: St. Anthony's.
College: Santa Clara.
Major League career: seven seasons (N.Y. Yankees 1954–55, Washington 1956–58, Boston 1958, Detroit 1959–60).

Berberet was a three-sport standout at St. Anthony's and went to Santa Clara on a football scholarship. A stocky, solid defensive catcher, he platooned for three seasons (1957, 1959–60) and had his best season in 1959 (thirteen home runs, forty-four RBIs) for the Tigers. He coached the 1963 Long Beach Peterson Post American Legion team and later became a college basketball and football official.

ROCKY BIDDLE / P / 6–3, 230 / R-R
Born: May 21, 1976, Las Vegas.
High School: Temple City.
College: Long Beach State.
Drafted: 1997, first, Chicago White Sox.
Major League career: five seasons (Chicago White Sox 2000–02, Montreal 2003–04).

Biddle won twenty games in his Dirtbag career and had 361 strikeouts, which stands second on the career all-time list behind Jered Weaver. He missed the 1999 season after having Tommy John surgery but bounced back in 2001 when he went 7–8 and started twenty-one games for the White Sox. He moved to the bullpen a year later and became Montreal's closer after being traded, posting thirty-four saves in seventy-three appearances. Elbow inflammation cut short his career.

NICK BIERBRODT / P / 6–5, 190 / L-L
Born: May 16, 1978, Tarzana.
High School: Millikan.
Drafted: 1996, first, Arizona.
Major League career: three seasons (Arizona 2001, Tampa 2001, 2003, Cleveland 2003, Texas 2004).

Bierbrodt was making progress in the Arizona system and was 6–2 in eleven starts in 2001 with a 1.75 ERA when he got the call to the majors. He was traded to Tampa and was on a 2002 rehab assignment in Charleston, South Carolina, when he was shot three times, once in the chest and twice in his right arm, while sitting in the back seat of a car at a fast food restaurant in what police called a random act of violence. He kept trying comebacks, including four years in independent ball and 2011 in the Mexico League.

EDDIE BOCKMAN / 3B / 5–9, 175 / R-R
Born: July 26, 1920, Santa Ana; Died: September 29, 2011.
High School: Wilson.
Major League career: four seasons (N.Y. Yankees 1946, Cleveland 1947, Pittsburgh 1947–48).

Bockman, a Wilson teammate of Lemon, signed with the Yankees and made his Major League debut in 1946, sharing a dugout with Joe DiMaggio, Phil Rizzuto, Bill Dickey, Yogi Berra, Joe Gordon, Charlie Keller and Tommy Henrich and wearing Babe Ruth's old No. 3. He spent 1947 as a teammate of Lemon's with the Indians and played with Ralph Kiner in Pittsburgh. He then spent four years playing in the PCL and another four years managing in the minors. It was just the beginning, though; he would spend the next forty-five years as a scout for the Philadelphia Phillies and Florida Marlins until he retired in 2003. He did yeoman work for the

Eddie Bockman served as a technical advisor and an extra in the film *The Stratton Story*, featuring legendary actor Jimmy Stewart.

Phillies. In the 1980 World Series, there were seven players on the roster that he scouted and signed: Larry Bowa, Bob Boone, Dick Ruthven, Bob Walk, George Vuckovich, Randy Lerch and Warren Brusstar. "It's been 65 years, my whole life, from the first day out of high school," Bockman said a few years before his passing. "And I enjoyed every bit of it. I was able to get into three World Series and win two, so I feel very lucky and very thankful. Especially when you see the players you signed get to the big leagues."

JOHN BOWKER / OF / 6–1, 205 / L-L
Born: July 8, 1983, Sacramento.
High School: Rio Americano (Sacramento).
College: Long Beach State.
Drafted: 2004, third round, San Francisco.
Major League career: four seasons (San Francisco 2008–10, Pittsburgh 2010–11, Philadelphia 2011).

Bowker led the Dirtbags in home runs in 2003 and 2004 and hit .323 in his career. He hit twenty-two home runs with ninety RBIs in the minors to earn a job in San Francisco in 2008, and he hit .255 with ten home runs in 111 games. He won the starting job in 2010 spring training but slumped in April and was traded to Pittsburgh. Bowker turned to Japan and in 2012 was part of the Yomiuri Giants' World Series champs. A late-season recall, he hit .303 with three home runs and ten RBIs and starred in the postseason.

MILTON BRADLEY / OF / 6–0, 180 / R-R
Born: April 15, 1978, Harbor City.
High School: Poly.
Drafted: 1996, second round, Montreal.
Major League career: twelve seasons (Montreal 2000–01, Cleveland 2001–03, L.A. Dodgers 2004–05, Oakland 2006–07, San Diego 2007, Texas 2008, Chicago Cubs 2009, Seattle 2010–11).

The fact that Bradley played for eight teams in a twelve-year career establishes Bradley's scorched-earth policy when it came to authority. He spent only three seasons with one team (Cleveland) and actually played less than a full season of games with six of the eight. He had an altercation with Manager Eric Wedge in Cleveland. In L.A., he had a sincere supporter in manager Jim Tracy but couldn't stop himself from throwing a plastic beer bottle at a fan, calling out Jeff Kent and getting into a near fistfight with a reporter. He was dumped by Oakland after some intemperate comments, he went after an umpire while with San

Diego (tearing his ACL and KO'ing his manager in the process), he tried to chase down an announcer while with Texas and had several run-ins with Cubs management. At the age of thirty-four, he was out of baseball in 2012. Bradley could never stay healthy, playing just 1,042 games in twelve seasons and playing in over 100 games just four times. He had his best season with Texas in 2008, with twenty-two home runs, seventy-seven RBIs and a .321 average. Those who saw him play at Poly believed they were seeing a star in the making; unfortunately, he went nova too soon.

JACK BREWER / P / 6–2, 170 / R-R
Born: April 21, 1918, Los Angeles; Died: November 30, 2003.
High School: Poly.
College: USC.
Major League career: three seasons (N.Y. Giants 1944–46).

Brewer appeared during the World War II era and had his busiest season in 1945 when he was 8–6 with a 3.83 ERA and eight complete games. He played four years in the PCL after his Major League days.

ROCKY BRIDGES / SS / 5–10, 175/ R-R
Born: August 7, 1925, Refugio (TX).
High School: Poly.
Major League career: eleven seasons (Brooklyn 1951–52, Cincinnati 1953–57, Washington 1957–1958, Detroit 1958–60, Cleveland 1960, St. Louis 1960, L.A. Angels 1961).

No one was more unique or jovial than Everett Lamar Bridges. He was a star on the Poly teams during World War II and signed by Bob Hughes for the Brooklyn Dodgers in 1947, becoming the first local kid to play for the iconic franchise. He was a versatile infielder and good enough to start in four seasons and in 1958 made the A.L. All-Star team while with the Senators. "I was hitting .307 at the break, then decided to try and catch a Frank Lary fastball with my jaw," Bridges said. He spent his last season in the majors with the expansion L.A. Angels. *Sports Illustrated* tagged him as "one of the best stand-up comics in the history of baseball." Example: Asked about Little League baseball, he said, "I think it's all right. It keeps parents off the streets." Bridges had a long post-playing career, serving as a coach for seven seasons, six with the Angels, and twenty-one years as a minor league manager, mostly in the Giants organization, where he won 1,300 games.

Ollie Brown / OF / 6–3, 200 / R-R
Born: February 11, 1944, Tulsa (OK).
High School: Poly.
Major League career: thirteen seasons (San Francisco 1965–68, San Diego 1969–72, Oakland 1972, Milwaukee 1972–73, Houston 1974, Philadelphia 1974–77).

Ollie's family was a foundation of Poly sports for more than a decade. Older brother Willie was a standout football and basketball player, and younger brother Oscar also played pro baseball. Brown credits many people for his success—Poly coach John Herbold, Giants minor league manager and scout Bill Werle and Hall of Famers Willie Mays and Willie McCovey. "I don't think I did as much for Long Beach as the city did for me," Brown said. "I couldn't have picked a better place when it came to the opportunities the city gave me and my family, being able to grow up in a place where there were good schools and plenty of sports programs for kids like me and my brothers." Brown had a breakout season in 1964 when he hit forty-three home runs for Fresno, the Giants' top affiliate. Brown was San Diego's first pick in the 1969 expansion draft, and he had his best seasons in San Diego, becoming the most popular player in franchise history until Tony Gwynn came along. He hit twenty home runs in 1969 and twenty-three with eighty-nine RBIs and a .292 average in 1970.

Oscar Brown / OF / 6–0, 175 / R-R
Born: February 8, 1946, Long Beach.
High School: Poly.
College: Compton College, USC.
Drafted: 1966, fifth round, Atlanta.
Major League career: five seasons (Atlanta 1969–73).

Oscar was younger and smaller than his brother. He went to college briefly to improve his draft status and hit .299 in the minors but was a reserve for the Braves in his five seasons, playing in just 160 games.

Jeff Burroughs / OF / 6–1, 200 / R-R
Born: March 7, 1951, Long Beach.
High School: Wilson.
Drafted: 1969, first round, Washington (first pick).
Major League career: seventeen seasons (Washington /Texas Rangers 1970–76, Atlanta 1977–80, Seattle 1981, Oakland 1982–84, Toronto 1985).

See chapter eight.

Sean Burroughs trades quips with *The Late Show*'s David Letterman after the 1993 LLWS win. *Bob Keisser collection.*

SEAN BURROUGHS / 3B / 6–2, 210 / L-R
Born: September 12, 1980, Atlanta.
High School: Wilson.
Drafted: 1998, first round, San Diego.
Major League career: seven seasons (San Diego 2002–05, Tampa Bay 2006, Arizona 2011, Minnesota 2012).

The first part of Burroughs's baseball life was every kid's dream. He led the Long Beach Little League to the World Series title in 1992 (Philippines won the title game but forfeited for ineligible players) and again in 1993, this time on the field. He starred at Wilson, was a first-round draft pick by the Padres and a member of the 2000 U.S. Olympic Games gold medal team. He was expected to be a star in San Diego, and he hit .271, .286 and .298 in his first three seasons. But he didn't hit for the kind of power expected from a third baseman. He was sent to the minors in 2005, traded in 2006 and left the game after a few minor league games in 2007. He dealt with depression and substance abuse for a few years in Las Vegas before turning his life around and was given a second chance by Arizona exec Kevin Towers, who drafted him in San Diego. He hit .273 in a backup role in 2011 and split 2012 between Minnesota and the minors.

RALPH BUXTON / P / 5–11, 163 / R-R
Born: June 7, 1911, Weyburn (Sasketchewan, Canada); Died: January 6, 1988.
High School: Poly.
Major League career: two seasons (Philadelphia A's 1938, N.Y. Yankees 1949).

Buxton's two Major League seasons came eleven years apart, with some yeoman and slightly soiled work in the PCL between them. He made five appearances with the A's in 1938 at the age of twenty-seven and then landed in the PCL with the Oakland Oaks, where he was known for putting pine tar on the crease of his pants or in his back pocket to enhance his sinker. His manager was Casey Stengel, and he won ninety-nine games in eight seasons. When Stengel became the Yankee manager, Buxton came with him and made fourteen appearances at the age of thirty-eight for the World Champs.

MIKE CARP / 1B / 6–2, 205 / L-R
Born: June 30, 1986, Long Beach.
High School: Lakewood.
Drafted: 2004, ninth round, N.Y. Mets.
Major League career: five seasons (Seattle 2009–12, Boston 2013).

Carp signed out of high school after starring for the Lancers and made it to Seattle in 2009. He got his first chance to play regularly in 2011 and hit .276 with twelve home runs and forty-six RBI. Injuries cut into his playing time in 2012, and he was dealt to Boston in the off-season.

ANDREW CARPENTER / P / 6–3, 240 / R-R
Born: May 18, 1985, Fairfield (CA).
High School: Vacaville.
College: Chico St., Sacramento CC, Long Beach State.
Drafted: 2006, second round, Philadelphia.
Major League career: five seasons (Philadelphia 2008–11, Pittsburgh 2011, Toronto 2012).

After a nice 7–4 season and 2.91 ERA in 2006, Carpenter was a surprise second round pick in the '06 draft. He has been on the fringe of the majors for five years, making twenty-three appearances but only getting one start.

WALTER CARSON / OF / 6–0, 180 / L-L
Born: November 15, 1912, Colton; Died: June 21, 1983.
High School: Poly.
Major League career: two seasons (Cleveland 1934–35).

"Kit" Carson hit .310 in nine minor league seasons but only got into twenty-one games in two seasons with the Indians, most of them as a pinch-hitter. He hit .250 in his brief career.

LARRY CASIAN / P / 6–0, 175/ R-L
Born: October 28, 1965, Lynwood.
High School: Lakewood.
College: Cal State–Fullerton.
Drafted: 1986, sixth round, Minnesota.
Major League career: nine seasons (Minnesota 1990–94, Cleveland 1994, Chicago Cubs 1995–97, Kansas City 1998, Chicago White Sox 1999).

Casian was the consummate left-handed specialist. He made 40 or more appearances in five seasons, pitching just 241 innings in 245 appearances, with just two career saves.

REX CECIL / P / 6–3, 195 / L-R
Born: October 8, 1916, Lindsay (OK); Died: October 30, 1966.
High School: Poly.
Major League career: two seasons (Boston 1944–45).

Cecil was 6–10 in two seasons with the Red Sox, one of the wins a complete game against the Yankees. He won 19 games in the minors three times and in his final season, 1951, won 21. He had 161 career minor league wins.

CRAIG CHAMBERLAIN / P / 5–1, 190 / R-R
Born: February 2, 1957, Hollywood.
High School: Los Alamitos.
College: Long Beach City College.
Drafted: 1978, first round, Kansas City.
Major League career: two seasons (Kansas City 1979–80).

Chamberlain was 16–2 and an all-state choice at LBCC and pitched complete game wins in his first three Major League starts, but his career yielded just twelve more appearances.

FLOYD CHIFFER / P / 6–2, 198 / R-R
Born: April 20, 1956, Glen Cove, New York.
High School: Lakewood.
College: UCLA.
Drafted: 1978, fifth round, San Diego.
Major League career: three seasons (San Diego 1982–84).

Chiffer made fifty-one appearances in 1982, more than his last two seasons combined. He had a decent 4.02 ERA for the era.

DICK COLE / IF / 6–2, 175 / R-R
Born: May 6, 1926, Long Beach.
High School: Wilson.
Major League career: six seasons (St. Louis 1951, Pittsburgh 1953–56, Milwaukee Braves 1957).

Cole was just seventeen when he made his pro debut with Sacramento in the PCL. He was in the Cardinals system for several years before being traded to the Pirates, where he was the everyday shortstop in 1954, hitting .270.

STEVE CONNELLY / P / 6–4, 210 / R-R
Born: April 27, 1974, Long Beach.
High School: Wilson.
College: Oklahoma.
Drafted: 1995, twenty-fourth round, Oakland.
Major League career: one season (Oakland 1998).

Connelly, a member of Oklahoma's 1994 CWS championship team, pitched in three games for the A's in 1998.

BRENT COOKSON / OF / 5–11, 200 / R-R
Born: September 7, 1969, Santa Paula (CA).
High School: Santa Paula.
College: Ventura College, Long Beach State.
Drafted: 1991, fifteenth round, Oakland.
Major League career: two seasons (Kansas City 1995, L.A. Dodgers 1999).

Cookson led the Dirtbags with 15 home runs in 1991 and hit 155 in a minor league career that saw him post a slash line of .293/.374/.548. He got very brief trials in the majors but also played in the Mexico League in 1997 and 2002–04 and briefly in Korea in 2003.

CASEY COX / P / 6–5, 200 / R-R
Born: July 3, 1941, Long Beach.
High School: Wilson.
College: Long Beach City College, Cal State–Los Angeles.
Major League career: eight seasons (Washington/Texas 1966–72, N.Y. Yankees 1972–73).

Cox filled a variety of roles in the majors, pitching in 120 games over 1966 and 1967, going 12–7 in 1969 as a swingman and 8–12 as a starter in 1970 and making fifty-four appearances in a dual role again in 1971.

Casey Cox (Wilson, Long Beach City College) had an eight-year pitching career with the Yankees and Washington Senators.

BOB CRAMER / P / 6–1, 205 / L-L
Born: October 28, 1979, Anaheim.
High School: Loara.
College: Fullerton CC, Long Beach State.
Major League career: two seasons (Oakland 2010–11).

Cramer pitched in just twenty-seven games for the Dirtbags over two seasons because of injuries and in 2002 underwent Tommy John surgery. He had a solid 2004 A-ball season for Tampa but was released and retired. In 2007, he launched a comeback and went 9–2 with a 2.77 ERA but was again released. He played Indy ball in 2008 and was headed to Italy in 2009 when the A's called again, and he finally reached AAA. In 2010, the A's arranged a sale of him to Quintana Roos in the Mexican League, where he was 13–3 with a 2.95 ERA, fifteen starts, five complete games and three shutouts. He was recalled by the A's and won his first start and finished 2–1 with a 3.04 ERA. He made five relief appearances for Oakland in 2011, but a strained elbow ended his season. In 2012, he was back on the road, playing for Quintana Roos as well as Yokohama in Japan.

BOBBY CROSBY / 2B / 6–3, 210 / R-R
Born: January 12, 1980, Lakewood.
High School: La Quinta.
College: Long Beach State.

Drafted: 2001, first, Oakland.
Major League career: seven seasons (Oakland 2003–09, Pittsburgh 2009, Arizona 2009).

The 2001 Big West player of the year hit .324 in his Dirtbag career with twenty-two home runs, ninety-two RBIs and a .324 average. By his third pro season, he was in the majors and winning A.L. Rookie of the Year honors in 2003 with twenty-two home runs and sixty-four RBIs. His career thereafter was besieged by injuries. The son of Ed Crosby only had more season with more than one hundred games played, in 2008, and he never matched his power totals.

Ed Crosby / SS / 6–2, 180 / L-R
Born: May 26, 1949, Long Beach.
High School: Wilson.
College: Long Beach City College.
Drafted: 1969, second round, St. Louis.
Major League career: six seasons (St. Louis 1970, Cincinnati 1973, Cleveland 1974–76).

Crosby played on the 1968–69 LBCC teams that won state titles. A superb defensive infielder, he filled a utility role for most of his six years except for 1972, when he was the starting second baseman for the Cards and got into 101 games. Crosby made his biggest mark in baseball as one of the best scouts on the West Coast and raised his own infielder who went on to become a Dirtbag and A.L. Rookie of the Year, Bobby Crosby.

Bud Daley / P / 6–1, 185 / L-L
Born: October 7, 1932, Orange.
High School: Wilson.
Major League career: ten seasons (Cleveland 1955–57, K.C. A's 1958–61, N.Y. Yankees 1961–64).

Daley pitched in two All-Star games and won two World Series with the New York Yankees. But the Wilson product said the 1950 CIF title he won at Wilson was his biggest thrill. Daley and Frank Followell pitched back-to-back no-hitters in the playoffs, and Daley drove in the winning run in a key playoff game. "People think I'm crazy when I say that," Daley said. "But can you imagine how big that was for a young baseball player? We had a great team, with seven or eight players eventually signing pro contracts." Daley, who had a slightly withered right arm, had a ten-year pro career with his left. He signed with Cleveland and was eventually traded in 1958 to the Kansas City A's, one of the most woebegone franchises in baseball. He won sixteen games in 1959 and sixteen more in 1960 and made the All-Star team both years. The Yankees obtained Daley in a 1961 mid-season trade. He pitched in twenty-three games with seventeen starts, winning eight. In Game 5 of the 1961 World Series, Daley relieved a struggling Ralph Terry in the third inning and went the rest of the way for the decision in the Yankees' series-clinching win. He pitched well in relief in 1962 as the Yankees won another title, beating the Giants in seven games. "When you pitched for Kansas City, you would think, 'I'm pitching for myself, for making the team the next year,'" he said. "When you pitched for the Yankees, you felt, 'If I don't win, I let this team down.'"

Wilson's Bud Daley made the American League All-Star team in 1959—the second game was played at the L.A. Coliseum—while with the Kansas City Athletics and got to be a teammate for a day with Red Sox great Ted Williams.

BENNIE DANIELS / P / 6–1, 193 / L-R
Born: June 17, 1932, Tuscaloosa (AL).
High School: Compton.
Major League career: nine seasons (1957–60 Pittsburgh, 1961–65 Washington).

Daniels, a three-sport star at Compton who was recruited to play basketball at UCLA, won eighty-three games in the minors, including seventeen with the Hollywood Stars in their last year of existence (1957). He lost two seasons to military service and had his best season with the Senators in 1961 (12–11, 3.44 ERA, twelve complete games) in 1961. He later worked at the Long Beach Veteran's Hospital.

BRAD DAVIS / C / 6–1, 190 / R-R
Born: December 29, 1982, San Diego.
High School: Capistrano Valley.
College: Long Beach State.
Drafted: 2005, fifth round, Florida.
Major League career: one season (Florida 2010).

Davis had a good college career, hitting .317 with two hundred hits, 102 runs and eighty-four RBIs, leading the 2003 team in hits and doubles. The Marlins recalled Davis at mid-season in 2010, and he split time behind the plate, hitting a grand slam to win a game 4–0.

Dick Davis / OF / 6–3, 195 / R-R
Born: September 25, 1953, Long Beach.
High School: Compton.
Major League career: six seasons (Milwaukee 1977–80, Philadelphia 1981–82, Toronto 1982, Pittsburgh 1982).

Davis hit twelve home runs for the Brewers in 1979 and .333 in forty-five games for the Phillies in 1981. He went to Japan after he was released and had a forty home run season.

Chris Demaria / P / 6–3, 210 / S-R
Born: September 28, 1980, Torrance.
High School: North Torrance.
College: El Camino College, Long Beach State.
Drafted: 2002, seventeenth round, Pittsburgh.
Major League career: two seasons (Kansas City 2005, Milwaukee 2006).

Demaria led the Dirtbags in appearances and ERA (2.98) in 2001. He had a career 2.84 minor league ERA with twenty-three wins and thirty-five saves in five seasons but had just eighteen relief dates in his two brief seasons in the majors.

Greg Dobbs / 3B-OF / 6–2, 210 / L-R
Born: July 2, 1978, Los Angeles.
High School: Canyon Springs, Carlsbad.
College: Riverside City College, Long Beach State, Oklahoma.
Major League career: ten seasons (Seattle 2004–06, Philadelphia 2007–10, Florida 2011–13).

Dobbs is often left off lists of Dirtbags in the majors because he parted company with the team after the 1999 season and transferred to Oklahoma. In 1999, he led Long Beach in average (.376) and hits (eighty-six) and drove in sixty-three runs. Undrafted after his senior season, he signed with Seattle and eventually made his way to Philadelphia, where he played 142 games and hit ten home runs with fifty-five RBIs in a super-sub role. He got a chance to play full time with the Marlins in 2011, hitting .275.

DAMION EASLEY / 2B-SS / 5–11, 195 / R-R
Born: November 11, 1969, New York.
High School: Lakewood.
College: Long Beach City College.
Drafted: 1988, thirtieth round, L.A. Angels.
Major League career: seventeen seasons (L.A. Angels 1992–96, Detroit 1996–2002, Tampa 2003, Florida 2004–05, Arizona 2006, N.Y. Mets 2007–08).

Easley led the Lancers to the 1987 CIF baseball title and two years later took Long Beach City College to the Southern California regional championship title game against Cerritos. He hit .320 as the team MVP that season, leading the team with eight home runs and being a second-team all-state selection. He was drafted by the Angels and made it to the majors in 1992. Injuries and the Angels' reluctance to give him a steady job slowed his progress, and in 1996, he was traded to Detroit, where he blossomed. He hit twenty-two, twenty-seven and twenty home runs over the next three seasons while driving in one hundred RBI in 1998. He credits his coaches for his success, Lakewood's Spud O'Neil and LBCC coach Ken Gaylord. "Spud wanted us to know how to bunt, how to hit and run, when to hit and run. I didn't realize how much he taught me about baseball until I got into the pros."

BRUCE ELLINGSEN / P / 6–0, 198/ L-L
Born: April 26, 1949, Pocatello, Idaho.
High School: Lakewood.
Drafted: 1967, sixty-third round, L.A. Dodgers.
Major League career: one season (Cleveland 1974).

Once considered a prospect with the Dodgers, Ellingsen only had one brief stay in the majors, with the Indians, when he was 1–1 in sixteen games.

DANNY ESPINOSA / 2B / 6–0, 205 / S-R
Born: April 21, 1987, Santa Ana.
High School: Mater Dei.
College: Long Beach State.
Drafted: 2008, third round, Washington.
Major League career: four seasons (Washington Nationals 2010–13).

Espinosa hit .309 in his Dirtbag career and was part of the long line of exceptional shortstops. He had 197 career hits and 123 runs and shared the team lead in home runs in 2007 with seven. Washington used him at shortstop in the minors but converted him to second base before the 2011 season, when he became an every day regular. He hit .236 with twenty-one home runs and sixty-six RBIs in 2011 and seventeen home runs and fifty-six RBIs in 2012.

Marco Estrada / P / 5–11, 200 / R-R
Born: July 5, 1983, Sonora, Mexico.
High School: Sylmar.
College: Glendale CC, Long Beach State.
Drafted: 2005 sixth round, Washington.
Major League career: six seasons (Washington Nationals 2008–09, Milwaukee 2010–13).

Estrada was a nice find by the Dirtbags, becoming the No. 2 starter behind Cesar Ramos while going 8–3 with a 2.43 ERA and leading the team in strikeouts (104) and walks (twenty-four). He got a small taste of the majors in his first three seasons before becoming a middle reliever for the Brewers in 2011 and then moving into the rotation in 2012, posting a 3.64 ERA.

Ron Fairly / 1B-OF / 5–10, 180 / L-L
Born: July 12, 1938, Macon, Georgia.
High School: Jordan.
College: USC.
Major League career: twenty-one seasons (L.A. Dodgers 1958–69, Montreal 1969–74, St. Louis 1975–76, Oakland 1976, Toronto 1977, L.A. Angels 1978).

See chapter eight.

Mike Fitzgerald / C / 5–11, 190 / R-R
Born: July 13, 1960, Long Beach.
High School: Lakewood.
Drafted: 1978, sixth round, N.Y. Mets.
Major League career: ten seasons (N.Y. Mets 1983–84, Montreal 1985–91, L.A. Angels 1972).

A three-year starter for John Herbold at Lakewood, he led the Lancers to a CIF title as a sophomore in 1976 and to the title game again in 1977. He is one of the few baseball players to hit a home run in his first Major League at bat, in September 1983. His parents didn't even know he had been called up, so they got the news the second-best way possible: hearing Vin Scully, during a Dodger broadcast, announce that Fitzgerald had just homered. He had a ten-year career in the majors, and it would have been longer if not for a finger injury. He was the Expos' starting catcher in 1986 and having a career year—.282, .364 on-base percentage, six home runs and thirty-seven RBIs—when a pitch in the dirt caught the index finger on his right hand on the tip, shattering two knuckles. A newspaper story after the injury said it looked like the finger had been blown apart with a grenade. Doctors recommended fusing two joints. He balked, had the knuckles rebuilt with cartilage and was able to resume his career. "One doctor said it was like trying to repair a broken potato chip, with all these little pieces," he said. "All I knew was that I wasn't going to quit, that I'd find a way to keep playing." In 1990, he had career highs in games, home runs and on-base percentage and led the National League in double plays by a catcher. Fitzgerald coached, briefly becoming an assistant at Cerritos Valley Christian High and then head coach for several years, winning a CIF title in 2003.

JOHN FLANNERY / IF / 6–3, 173 / R-R
Born: January 25, 1957, Long Beach.
High School: Lakewood.
Drafted: 1975, ninth round, L.A. Angels.
Major League career: one season (L.A. Angels 1977).

Flannery was a two-time All-CIF pick at Lakewood but played in just seven games and got two at-bats in 1977. He's been a Major League scout for upwards of two decades.

DAVE FROST / P / 6–6, 235 / R-R
Born: November 17, 1952, Long Beach.
High School: Millikan.
College: Long Beach City College, Stanford.
Drafted: 1974, eighteenth round, Chicago White Sox.
Major League career: six seasons (Chicago White Sox 1977, L.A. Angels 1978–81, Kansas City 1982).

Frost had a great high school and college career—a CIF baseball title in 1969, a CIF basketball title in 1970 under Howard Lyon and a state title at Long Beach City College for Lute Olson. That earned him a scholarship at Stanford and a Major League shot when he was drafted in 1974 by the White Sox. "It all started with Bob Seymour when he was my basketball coach at Stanford Junior High School," Frost said. "He was tremendous, and taught me so much. And then at Millikan I was blessed to have Bob Myers as my baseball coach and Lyon as my basketball coach. And then I go to Long Beach City College, and have the legendary Joe Hicks coaching me in baseball and a future legendary coach in Olson in basketball. I had terrific mentors. An even though my dad [Wally] was in a wheelchair, he would hit me ground balls with a sawed off bat and teach me about the game when I was a kid." His career flourished in the four seasons he was with the Angels, going 16–10 with a 3.57 ERA in 1979 and helping the Angels to their first-ever postseason appearance. He was prepping for a big 1980 when he suffered elbow pain, and tests showed he had fourteen bone chips floating in his elbow, bringing his career to a premature end.

Frank Gabler / P / 6–1, 175 / R-R
Born: November 6, 1911, East Highland (CA); Died: January 1, 1967.
High School: Poly.
Major League career: four seasons (New York Giants 1935–37, Boston Braves 1937–38, Chicago White Sox 1938).

"The Great Gabbo" earned his nickname for his non-stop chatter and self-effacing manner. He almost had his career, and life, end before he reached the majors. He suffered a skull fracture when hit in the head pitching for Kansas City in 1934. But he made the Giants roster in 1935 and in 1936 went 9–8 with a 3.12 ERA in forty-three games, making two relief appearances in the '36 World Series against the Yankees. He had five complete games in fourteen starts and six saves.

Mike Gallo / P / 6–0, 180 / L-L
Born: April 2, 1977, Long Beach.
High School: Millikan.
College: Long Beach City College, Long Beach State.
Drafted: 1999, fifth round, Houston.
Major League career: four seasons (Houston 2003–06).

"Pepe" is one of the most popular players in town, having won the local triple crown by playing high school, JC and college ball in Long Beach. He had his peak years in the 1998 and 1999 seasons at Long Beach State, where the Dirtbags advanced to the College World Series in '98 and Gallo went 10–3 in '99. The Astros drafted him with plans to start him, but he was moved to the bullpen in his third pro season and never escaped the left-handed specialist role. He made 160 appearances with the Astros but pitched just 115 innings. He had a 2.66 ERA in 2005, when the Astros made it to their first World Series. He made 10 postseason appearances and had a 1.69 ERA.

NOMAR GARCIAPARRA / SS / 6–0, 175 / R-R
Born: July 23, 1973, Whittier.
High School: St. John Bosco (Bellflower).
College: Georgia Tech.
Drafted: 1994, first round, Boston.
Major League career: fourteen seasons (Boston 1996–2004, Chicago Cubs 2004–05, L.A. Dodgers 2006–08, Oakland 2009).

His father's name was Ramon, so Dad reversed the spelling for his son. He already had a live bat in high school, was an All-American at Georgia Tech and was mentioned in every discussion about the great active shortstops with Derek Jeter and Alex Rodriguez for years. He was beloved in Boston before a contractual falling-out with management. Nomar won two batting titles, had a six-hit game, a 9-RBI game and, in a four-year period (1997–2000), had 113 home runs, 420 RBIs, fifty-three steals, 174 doubles and scored 103 runs or more each season. He had a one-year revival with the hometown Dodgers in 2008, hitting .303 with 20 home runs and 93 RBIs.

ROD GASPAR / OF / 5–11, 165 / S-R
Born: April 3, 1946, Long Beach.
High School: Lakewood.
College: Long Beach City College, Long Beach State.
Drafted: 1967, second round, N.Y. Mets.
Major League career: four seasons (N.Y. Mets 1969–71, San Diego 1974).

Gaspar went to Lakewood and played a year at Long Beach City College and three at Long Beach State, where he hit .393 in 1966 for Bob Wuesthoff's team and led the team in hits, runs and doubles in 1967. He went to the Mets training camp in 1969 as a long shot to make a roster that included outfielders Cleon Jones, Tommie Agee, Ron Swoboda and Art Shamsky. But manager Gil Hodges liked his versatility, and he made the team. Gaspar started the season opener in right field. He had two hits, a walk, an RBI, a steal and scored a run, and he was seven for seventeen in his first four games. "It all started with Hodges," Gaspar said. "He did a great job with a bunch of young kids. We only had a few veterans on the team, and he used his roster the best way possible. He didn't wear any of us out. He gave young guys a chance to contribute." The Miracle Mets won, much to the surprise of those who remember their early futility as a 1962 expansion team. Gaspar's World Series moment came in Game 4 against the Baltimore Orioles, when he scored the game winner from second when the Orioles threw away a sacrifice bunt.

Jason Giambi / 1B-DH / 6–3, 250 / L-R
Born: January 8, 1971, West Covina.
High School: South Hills.
College: Long Beach State.
Drafted: 1992, second round, Oakland.
Major League career: nineteen seasons (Oakland 1995–2001, 2009, N.Y. Yankees 2002–08, Colorado 2009–12, Cleveland 2013).

See chapter eleven.

Chris Gomez / SS / 6–1, 195 / R-R
Born: June 6, 1971, Los Angeles.
High School: Lakewood.
College: Loyola Marymount, Long Beach State.
Drafted: 1992, third round, Detroit.
Major League career: sixteen seasons (Detroit 1993–96, San Diego 1996–2001, Tampa 2001–02, Minnesota 2003, Toronto 2004, Baltimore 2005–07, Cleveland 2007, Pittsburgh 2008).

Gomez left Loyola Marymount for Long Beach State after the Lions dawdled on a coaching change. He got the chance to play for Dave Snow, was invited to the 1992 U.S. Olympic baseball training camp, earned All-American honors and was drafted by the Tigers. He was called up to the majors on July 19, 1993, after a few months of playing time at AAA Toledo. Gomez would play sixteen seasons, becoming the Tigers' starter in 1995 and hitting eleven home runs. He was traded to San Diego in 1996 and was the Padres everyday starter for three years, including 1998, when he hit .267 on the season and .346 in the final forty-two games to help the Pads to the World Series. That was his major thrill in his career. "Playing in the World Series against the New York Yankees. Starting at shortstop. The games on national television. All I ever wanted as a kid growing up in Lakewood was to play major league ball." Even after the Padres cut him loose, he would continue to find work, playing for six teams between 2001 and 2008 and becoming a starter in 2002 with Tampa and 2004 with Toronto, where he hit .282.

Gabe Gonzalez / P / 6–1, 160 / S-L
Born: May 24, 1972, Long Beach.
High School: Wilson.
College: Long Beach State.
Drafted: 1996, sixteenth round, Florida.
Major League career: one season (Florida 1998).

Nicknamed "Blade" by Dirtbag coach Dave Snow because he was so tall and thin, Gonzalez is the best reliever in Long Beach State history, holding school records for career and single season appearances and saves (forty-six career, twenty in 1995). Gonzalez had exceedingly good control and a nice sinker and moved into a closer role as a freshman. He was being fitted for a reliever role in Florida and made the opening day roster in 1998 but got into only three games before going back to the minors.

JACK GRAHAM / 1B / 6–2, 200 / L-L
Born: December 24, 1916, Minneapolis, Minnesota; Died: December 30, 1998.
High School: Wilson.
Major League career: two seasons (N.Y. Giants 1946, St. Louis Browns 1949).
See chapter thirteen.

CRAIG GREBECK / SS-2B / 5–7, 155 / R-R
Born: December 29, 1964, Johnstown, Pennsylvania.
High School: Lakewood.
College: Cal State–Dominguez Hills.
Major League career: twelve seasons (Chicago White Sox 1990–95, Florida 1996, L.A. Angels 1997, Toronto 1998–2000, Boston 2001).

Grebeck was a five foot six, 135-pound shortstop at Lakewood and undrafted as a high school player. He was a Division II All-American at Cal State–Dominguez Hills and was again undrafted out of college. John Herbold got him a look by a pro, and he took it from there. "Size is a big thing until you sign. Once you're in, if you produce, you play. If you work hard, do your job, keep your mouth shut and keep your nose clean, you can make it," Grebeck said. In 1991, he got the chance to be the White Sox starting shortstop and hit .281 with a .386 on-base percentage while driving in thirty-one runs replacing injured starter Ozzie Guillen. He would get a chance to start in 1998 in Toronto, too, and became a valuable defensive option for eleven seasons. He hit over .270 in five of those seasons and .261 for his career, with career fielding percentages of .981 at second base and .973 at short.

BOBBY GRICH / 2B / 6–2, 190 / R-R
Born: January 15, 1949, Muskegon, Michigan.
High School: Wilson.
Drafted: 1967, first round, Baltimore.
Major League career: seventeen seasons (Baltimore 1970–76, L.A. Angels 1977–86).
See chapter five.

Chris Gwynn / OF / 6–0, 210/ L-L
Born: October 13, 1964, Los Angeles.
High School: Poly.
College: San Diego State.
Drafted: 1985, first round, L.A. Dodgers.
Major League career: ten seasons (L.A. Dodgers 1987–91, 1994–95, Kansas City 1992–93, San Diego 1996).

Tony Gwynn's younger brother had the more impressive high school baseball career at Poly (.482 as a senior) and was a first-round pick by the Dodgers out of San Diego State. Like his brother, he hit well for average but never for the kind of power anticipated for a stocky outfielder. He hit .284 for the Dodgers in 1990 and finally got a chance to play everyday when he went to K.C. In 1993, he was hitting .300 before an injury ended his season. He had the game-winning double in the eleventh inning of the 1996 regular season finale against the Dodgers to give the Padres the N.L. West title and added two hits in the playoffs. His last hit was a single in Game 2, and he scored on a follow-up single by his brother. Tony Gwynn says watching Chris get the game-winning hit against the Dodgers is one of the greatest thrills of his life. Until that season, he and Chris had never played on the same organized team. "It's my brother, we're playing for the pennant and a playoff spot, and it's against the team we both loved growing up and in the stadium where we spent so much time," he said. "It doesn't get any better than that." Gwynn has worked in scouting and player personnel since retiring.

Tony Gwynn / OF / 5–11, 200 / L-L
Born: May 9, 1960, Los Angeles.
High School: Poly.
College: San Diego State.
Drafted: 1981, third round, San Diego.
Major League career: twenty seasons (San Diego 1982–2001).

See chapter three.

Greg Harris / P / 6–0, 165 / R-R
Born: November 2, 1955, Lynwood.
High School: Los Alamitos.
College: Long Beach City College.
Drafted: 1976, seventh round, N.Y. Mets.
Major League career: fifteen seasons (N.Y. Mets 1981; Cincinnati 1982–83; Montreal 1984, 1995; San Diego 1984; Texas 1985–87; Philadelphia 1988–89; Boston 1989–94; N.Y. Yankees 1994).

Harris was a well-traveled, workaholic middle reliever for eight teams in his long career that included seventy-four wins, fifty-four saves and a 3.69 ERA. He hit his stride in the mid-'80s, having eleven saves and a 2.47 ERA in fifty-nine games with Texas and twenty saves, ten wins and a 2.83 ERA a year later. His longest stay was with the Red Sox for six years, and he did some of his best work there. In 1990, Boston moved him to the rotation, and he made thirty starts while going 13–9. He was a swingman in 1991 and then went back to the bullpen and made a career-high eighty appearances in 1993. Harris taught himself to throw left-handed during his career. "It's normal for me in the off-season. I always use both arms. To me, throwing left-handed saves the right," he said. The Expos allowed him to pitch an inning with both hands in 1995, walking one and not allowing a hit. He was the first player to throw with both hands since Tony Mullane in 1893.

Bobby Henrich / IF / 6–1, 185 / R-R
Born: December 24, 1938, Lawrence, Kansas.
High School: Compton.
Major League career: three seasons (Cincinnati 1957–59).

Henrich, a distant relation of former Yankee great Tommy Heinrich, had fielding skills and was eighteen years old when he made his debut, but he received just sixteen at-bats in his forty-eight games for the Reds.

Aaron Hicks / OF / 6–2, 190 / S-R
Born: October 2, 1989, San Pedro.
High school: Wilson.
Drafted: 2008, first round, Minnesota.
Major League career: one season (Minnesota 2013).

Hicks has been one of the Twins' top prospects since signing out of high school, had a breakout year in 2012 and is the latest local to reach the majors, starting the 2013 season as the Twins' center fielder.

Aaron Holbert / SS / 6–0, 160 / R-R
Born: January 9, 1973, Torrance.
High School: Jordan.
Drafted: 1990, first round, St. Louis.
Major League career: two seasons (St. Louis 1996, Cincinnati 2005).

Aaron was a shortstop like his older brother, Ray, and reached the majors in his seventh pro season with the Cardinals, but he played in just one game. He spent the next nine seasons playing AAA ball for eight different organizations, stealing 310 bases, before getting a second shot nine years later, in 2005, for twenty-two games with the Reds.

Ray Holbert / SS / 6–0, 175 / R-R
Born: September 25, 1970, Torrance.
High School: Jordan.
Drafted: 1988, third round, San Diego.
Major League career: five seasons (San Diego 1994–95, Atlanta 1998, Montreal 1998, Kansas City 1999–2000).

The elder Holbert was a top prospect in the Padres system who never hit well enough to stick, getting just 202 at-bats in five partial seasons. When he did get a limited chance to play in 1999, he hit .270 with seven steals.

Leon Hooten / P / 5–11, 180 / R-R
Born: April 4, 1948, Downey.
High School: Jordan.
College: Long Beach City College, Arizona.
Major League career: one season (Oakland 1974).

Hooten got into six games in 1974 with the A's, had his best minor league season in 1975 (15–11) and was out of baseball after 1976.

Gail Hopkins / 1B / 5–10, 200 / L-R
Born: February 19, 1943, Tulsa, Oklahoma.
High School: Jordan.
College: Pepperdine.
Major League career: seven seasons (Chicago White Sox 1968–70, Kansas City 1971–73, L.A. Dodgers 1974).

Hopkins was a light-hitting first baseman whose best seasons came at the height of the modern deadball era. In 1968, he hit .265 with eight home runs, hit .286 in 116 games in 1970 and .279 with nine home runs in 1971. After a brief stay with the Dodgers, he signed to play in Japan and led Hiroshima to its first Japan League title.

Jared Hughes / P / 6–7, 245 / R-R
Born: July 4, 1985, Stamford, Connecticut.
High School: Santa Margarita.
College: Santa Clara, Long Beach State.
Drafted: 2006, fourth round, Pittsburgh.
Major League career: three seasons (Pittsburgh 2011–13).

Hughes was 16–7 with a 3.29 ERA in two years and led the 2006 team with eight wins. He was a starter in five minor league seasons before the Bucs began transitioning him to relief. In 2012, he made sixty-six appearances with a 2.85 ERA as a middle man.

MARCUS JONES / P / 6–5, 235 / R-R
Born: March 29, 1975, Bellflower.
High School: Esperanza.
College: Long Beach State.
Drafted: 1997, third round, Oakland.
Major League career: one season (Oakland 2000).

Jones was a durable four-year letterman who won nine games with a 3.73 ERA in 1997, a year after eleven wins. He's fifth all-time in career starts, tied for fifth in career wins (twenty-three) and third in strikeouts (297). Jones made a start in 2000, the same year he developed arm trouble.

ODELL JONES / P / 6–3, 175 / R-R
Born: June 13, 1953, Tulare, California.
High School: Compton.
College: Compton College.
Major League career: nine seasons (Pittsburgh 1975, 1977–78, 1981; Seattle 1979; Texas 1983–84; Baltimore 1986; Milwaukee 1988).

Jones had 112 minor league wins and bounced around pro ball for fifteen seasons, nine of them in the majors. He made thirty-four appearances for the Pirates in 1977, had nineteen starts for the M's in 1979 and had his best season in 1983 with Texas, getting ten saves with a 3.09 ERA in forty-two games.

DENNIS LAMP / P / 6–3, 200 / R-R
Born: September 23, 1952, Los Angeles.
High School: St. John Bosco (Bellflower).
Drafted: 1971, third round, Chicago Cubs.
Major League career: sixteen seasons (Chicago Cubs 1977–80, Chicago White Sox 1981–83, Toronto 1984–86, Oakland 1987, Boston 1988–91, Pittsburgh 1992).

Lamp was a durable pitcher who filled a lot of roles in his career, opening it as a starter for five years in Chicago before being turned into a reliever in 1983, with seven wins and fifteen saves in forty-nine games. He had eight wins and nine saves in 1994 and was a perfect 11–0 in 1985. Lamp, whose brother Kevin caught at Long Beach State, finished his career with ninety-six wins and a 3.93 ERA.

DON LANG / 3B / 6–0, 175 / R-R
Born: March 15, 1915, Selma, California; Died: September 1, 2010.
High School: Poly.
Major League career: two seasons (Cincinnati 1938, St. Louis 1948).

Lang got a cup of coffee with the Reds in 1938 and waited another decade for a second sip. An injury to Whitey Kurowski led the Cards to give Lang the third base job, and he hit .269 with a .364 on-base percentage while leading the N.L. in fielding.

LYN LARY / SS / 6–0, 165 / R-R
Born: January 28, 1906, Armona, California; Died, January 9, 1973.
High School: Poly.
Major League career: twelve seasons (N.Y. Yankees 1929–34; Boston 1934; Washington 1935; St. Louis Browns 1935–36, 1940; Cleveland 1937–39; Brooklyn 1939; St. Louis 1939).

SABR's bio project and the first edition of *Who's Who in Baseball* (1933) say Lary's family moved to Southern California and he graduated from Poly, but there's no record of him playing for the Jackrabbits. Lary was a solid shortstop who hit .281 with fifty-four extra-base hits and 107 RBI in 1931, and he led the A.L. in steals in 1936 with thirty-seven. He was well traveled after leaving the Yankees, playing for six franchises in his final seven seasons.

BOB LEMON / P, manager / 6–0, 195 / L-R
Born: September 22, 1920, San Bernardino; Died: January 11, 2000
High School: Wilson.
Major League career: thirteen seasons (Cleveland 1946–58). As manager: nine seasons (K.C. 1970–72; Chicago White Sox 1977–78; N.Y. Yankees 1978–79, 1981–82).

See chapter two.

JEFF LIEFER / OF-1B / 6–3, 195 / L-R
Born: August 17, 1974, Fontana.
High School: Upland.
College: Long Beach State.
Drafted: 1995, first, Chicago White Sox.

Major League career: seven seasons (Chicago White Sox 1999–02, Montreal 2003, Tampa 2003, Milwaukee 2004, Cleveland 2005).

Liefer was a three-year starter, leading the team in hits in 1993 as a freshman and helping the Dirtbags to the CWS. He was nine for eighteen in the CWS with two home runs. He led the team in RBIs with 50 in 1994 and in 1995 led the team in average (.354), hits, home runs (thirteen) and RBIs (56). He's first in career home runs (thirty) and total bases, second in RBIs (160) and doubles (fifty-two) and third in hits (230). He hit twenty-two home runs in the minors in 1998 and thirty-two in 2000 and then had a breakout year with the White Sox in 2001, hitting eighteen home runs with 39 RBI in just 254 at-bats. His numbers fell in 2002, and he was traded to Montreal. He continued to mash in the minors, hitting twenty homers in 2004 and nineteen in 2005 but couldn't make a dent in the majors. He played two seasons in Japan and then retired after one last minor league season in 2008.

EVAN LONGORIA / 3B / 6-2, 190 / R-R
Born: October 7, 1985, Downey.
High School: St. John Bosco (Bellflower).
College: Rio Hondo, Long Beach State.
Drafted: 2006, first round, Tampa.
Major League career: six seasons (Tampa 2008–2013).

Longoria wasn't drafted or pursued out of high school but physically matured in his one season of JC ball and then blasted on the scene at Long Beach State, hitting eleven home runs while hitting .353 with the Dirtbags in 2006. He was rookie of the year in 2008 with twenty-seven home runs and followed that with thirty-three, twenty-two and thirty-one the next three seasons. He was limited to seventy-four games in 2012 but still hit seventeen home runs.

CLIFF MAPES / OF / 6-3, 205/ L-R
Born: March 3, 1922, Sutherland, Nebraska. Died: December 5, 1996.
High School: Jordan.
Major League career: five seasons (N.Y. Yankees 1948–51, St. Louis Browns 1951, Detroit 1952).

The strapping Mapes signed out of high school and spent six years in the minors and two years in the military before reaching the majors with the Yankees in '48. In 1950, he had more than four hundred at bats and twelve home runs with sixty-one RBIs and then was traded to the Browns in 1951. He earned World Series rings with the Yankees in 1949 and 1950. He holds the distinction of replacing a slumping Joe DiMaggio in the Yankee lineup in 1950; filling in for an injured Mickey Mantle in 1951; and wearing historic jersey numbers twice. He was wearing No. 3 at the time the Yankees chose to retire Babe Ruth's number. He switched to No. 7, forcing a young Mantle to wear number 6 until Mapes was traded.

DAVE MARSHALL / OF / 6-1, 190 / L-R
Born: January 14, 1943, Artesia.
High School: Lakewood.
College: Long Beach City College.
Major League career: six seasons (San Francisco 1967-69, N.Y. Mets 1970-72, San Diego 1973).

Marshall was the first Lancer four-sport letterman and the first to reach the majors, playing alongside Willie Mays in San Francisco and for Gil Hodges and Yogi Berra while with the New York Mets. He spent one year at Long Beach City College before signing with the Angels. A rotator cuff injury suffered in the minors hampered him defensively his entire career. "In those days, they didn't have the surgical procedures that they do now for torn rotator cuffs," he said. "I'll never forget going to see Dr. Robert Kerlan [then the Dodgers team doctor] and him telling me, 'There's nothing we can do.' So I took a lot of cortisone shots and a lot of pain pills. It definitely took away my power." Highlights of his seven-year career included hitting a grand slam home run off Gaylor Perry, being hit three straight times by Bob Gibson and getting eighth-inning hits to break up two no-hitters by Don Drysdale.

JIM MARSHALL / 1B, manager / 6-1, 190 / L-L
Born: May 25, 1931, Danville, Illinois.
High School: Compton.
College: Compton College.
Major League career: five seasons (Baltimore 1958, Chicago Cubs 1958–59, San Francisco Giants 1960–61, N.Y. Mets 1962, Pittsburgh 1962). As manager: Four seasons (Chicago Cubs 1974–76, Oakland 1979).

Marshall was a minor league standout for seven years, hitting 202 home runs, including two 30-plus seasons with Oakland in the Pacific Coast League, before he finally got the call from the majors. He had 11 home runs for the Cubs in 1959, backed up Willie McCovey and Orlando Cepeda for two seasons in San Francisco and played for the expansion Mets in 1962. He was traded six times. He later managed in the majors for four years, three with the Cubs and one in Oakland, and played three seasons and coached three seasons in Japan.

PAUL MCANULTY / OF-1B / 5-11, 225 / L-R
Born: February 21, 1981, Oxnard.
High School: Oxnard.
College: Oxnard CC, Long Beach State.
Drafted: 2002, twelfth round, San Diego.
Major League career: five seasons (San Diego 2005–08, L.A. Angels 2010).

McAnulty hit .369 with 9 homers and fifty-five RBIs in 2002, his only season at Long Beach. His best pro season was 2008 when he got 135 at-bats. He's been a steady producer in AAA, with a /.294/.383/.495 slash line and 171 home runs in twelve seasons, nine in AAA.

BRIAN MCCALL / OF / 5-10, 170 / L-L
Born: January 25, 1943, Kentfield, California.
High School: Poly.
Major League career: two seasons (Chicago White Sox 1962–63).

McCall made his debut as a nineteen-year-old in 1962 but got into only seven games with the White Sox.

JAMES MCDONALD / P / 6-5, 195 / L-R
Born: October 19, 1984, Long Beach.
High School: Poly.
College: Golden West.
Drafted: 2002, eleventh round, L.A. Dodgers.
Major League career: six seasons (L.A. Dodgers 2008–10, Pittsburgh 2011–13).

McDonald was drafted as a pitcher, moved to the outfield for two seasons and then returned to the mound, finally getting a late trial with the Dodgers in 2008. He worked well in relief in 2009 before being traded. He's won twenty-five in three seasons with the Pirates, including 12–8 in 2012.

ANDY MESSERSMITH / P / 6-1, 200 / R-R
Born: August 6, 1945, Toms River, New Jersey.
High School: Wilson, Western.
College: Cal Berkeley.
Drafted: 1966, first round, L.A. Angels.
Major League career: twelve seasons (L.A. Angels 1968–72, L.A. Dodgers 1973–75, 1979, Atlanta 1976-77, N.Y. Yankees 1978).

Messersmith started high school at Wilson, but the family moved and he transferred to Western High School. Messersmith had two twenty-win seasons, 1971 with the Angels and 1974 with the Dodgers, but he is best remembered as one of the first free agents in baseball history. He didn't produce much for the Braves, going 16–15 in two seasons.

RANDY MOFFITT / P / 6-3, 190 / R-R
Born: October 13, 1948, Long Beach.
High School: Poly.
College: Long Beach State.
Drafted: 1970, first round, San Francisco.
Major League career: twelve seasons (San Francisco 1972–81, Houston 1982, Toronto 1983).

See chapter eight.

CARLOS MUNIZ / P / 6-1, 190 / R-R
Born: March 12, 1981, Torrance.
High School: Banning.
College: L.A. Harbor, Long Beach State.
Drafted: 2003, thirteenth round, N.Y. Mets.
Major League career: two seasons (N.Y. Mets, 2007–08).

Muniz was the 49er closer in 2003, saving eleven games, and had the staff lowest ERA in 2002 (1.52). He had eighteen appearances for the Mets in 2008. He had 103 minor league saves and played in Mexico in 2011.

TONY MUSER / 1B, manager / 6-2, 190 / L-L
Born: August 1, 1947, Los Angeles.
High School: Lakewood.
College: San Diego Mesa.
Major League career: nine seasons (Boston 1969, Chicago White Sox 1971–75, Baltimore 1975–77, Milwaukee 1978). As manager: six seasons (Kansas City 1997–2002).

Muser was a good hitter and started four seasons, despite hitting just seven career home runs. He went into coaching after his playing career and became the third area player to become a Major League manager, with the Kansas City Royals from 1997 to 2002. He survived a harrowing experience in 1986: he was in Milwaukee's spring training locker room when there was a natural gas explosion. He suffered second- and third-degree burns over 55 percent of his body and was incapacitated for four months but returned to coaching the same year.

DICK NEN / 1B / 6-2 200 / L-L
Born: September 24, 1939, South Gate.
High School: Banning.
College: Long Beach State.
Major League career: six seasons (L.A. Dodgers 1963; Washington 1965–67, 1970; Chicago Cubs 1968).

Nen spent one season at Long Beach, leading the team in home runs and RBI (4/36), before signing with the Dodgers. He was a late-season call-up in 1963 while the Dodgers were fighting for the N.L. Pennant. In his first game on September 18, he hit a home run in the ninth inning to draw the Dodgers even with the Cardinals 5–5, and they won in thirteen innings. It would be his only hit as a Dodger. He spent '64 in the minors and at season's end was traded to Washington. He is the father of former Los Alamitos star Robb Nen.

CARL NICHOLS / C / 6-0, 184 / R-R
Born: October 10, 1962, Los Angeles.
High School: Compton.
Drafted: 1980, fourth round, Baltimore.
Major League career: six seasons (Baltimore 1986–88, Houston 1989–91).

Nichols was a strong-armed catcher who threw out more than 40 percent of all thieves. He was a reserve in all six seasons in the majors, playing in ninety-six games.

WILLIE NORWOOD / OF / 6-0, 185 / R-R
Born: November 7, 1950, Green County (AL)
High School: Poly.
College: LaVerne.
Drafted: 1972, third round, Minnesota.
Major League career: four seasons (Minnesota 1977–80).

Norwood got into 125 games for the Twins in 1978, hitting eight home runs with forty-six RBIs and twenty-five steals. He played two seasons in Mexico after the Twins released him.

SYD O'BRIEN / 3B / 6-1, 185 / R-R
Born: December 18, 1944, Compton.
High School: Millikan.
College: Long Beach City College.
Major League career: four seasons (Boston 1969, Chicago White Sox 1970, L.A. Angels 1971–72, Milwaukee 1972).

O'Brien signed as an undrafted free agent out of LBCC and got one extended trial in the majors, starting at third for the White Sox in 1970 while hitting .244 with eight home runs.

JIM PAGLIARONI / C / 6-4, 210 / R-R
Born: December 8, 1937, Dearborn, Michigan; Died: April 3, 2010.
High School: Wilson.
Major League career: eleven seasons (Boston 1955, 1960–62; Pittsburgh 1963–67; Oakland 1968–69; Seattle Pilots 1969).

Pagliaroni signed his pro contract before his high school season ended at Wilson, and as a "bonus baby" of the era—he signed for $75,000—he had to be placed on the Pirates roster, at the age of seventeen. He got one at-bat in 1955 and had a sacrifice fly. "He was an outstanding young player, very strong-armed catcher with good defense and some power," said Harry Minor, the former Bruin and Major League scout. Pags had good tools and enough power to hit double-digit home runs in six seasons and might have hit more if he hadn't been platooned as much as he was. In 1961, he had sixteen homers and fifty-eight RBIs for the Red Sox. He hit .295 for the Pirates in 1964 and has career highs of seventeen home runs and sixty-five RBIs in 1965. Pags was the on-deck hitter when Ted Williams hit his final home run in his last at-bat in 1960 and shook the Hall of Famer's hand as he crossed home plate. "He was a great player and a gracious individual," Pagliaroni said in the 2002 interview. "He helped me change my swing in 1960. I would catch behind Ted in spring training and you'd go to squeeze the glove because you figured you were going to catch the ball, only to have Ted hit it. He had those great wrists and arms and could wait until the last split second to swing." He also caught two no-hitters, including Catfish Hunter's perfect game in Oakland in 1968, and earned some notoriety as a member of the 1969 expansion Seattle Pilots, the setting for Jim Bouton's renowned book *Ball Four*.

BOB PATE / OF / 6-3, 200 / R-R
Born: December 3, 1953, Los Angeles.
High School: Compton.
College: San Diego Mesa, Arizona State.
Drafted: 1976, fourth round, Montreal.
Major League career: two seasons (Montreal 1980–81).

Pate had two brief appearances with the Expos, playing in thirty-one games.

Shane Peterson / 1B / 6-0, 210 / L-L
Born: February 11, 1988, Fallbrook.
High School: Chaparral.
College: Long Beach State.
Drafted: 2008, second round, St. Louis.
Major League career: one season (Oakland 2013).

Peterson led the team in average (. 390), hits (eighty-three), runs (fifty-two) and doubles in 2008 while also becoming the first player in school history to hit for the cycle in a game (2009). He had a twenty-two-game hitting streak in 2007. Oddly, he was recruited as a pitcher. He had a line of .326/.460/.510 in the 2012 minors and got an April recall by the A's in 2013.

Dante Powell / OF / 6-2, 195 / R-R
Born: August 25, 1973, Long Beach.
High School: Millikan.
College: Cal State–Fullerton.
Drafted: 1994, first round, San Francisco.
Major League career: four seasons (San Francisco 1997–99, Arizona 2001).

Powell falls into the category of fine talents who somehow never got a chance to show them. He hit twenty-six home runs and stole 109 bases at Fullerton and was on his way after a season in 1996 with twenty-one home runs, seventy-eight RBIs, forty-three steals and .280 at the AA level. But the Giants never gave him a full trial—twenty-seven, eight and thirteen games in three stints and twenty-two with Arizona in a fourth.

Cesar Ramos / P / 6-2, 205 / L-L
Born: June 22, 1984, Los Angeles.
High School: El Rancho.
College: Long Beach State.
Drafted: 2005, first round, San Diego.
Major League career: five seasons (San Diego 2009–10, Tampa 2011–13).

Ramos had an exceptional career, going 28–15 in three seasons with a 2.56 ERA. He was 6–4 in 2003 (2.85), 12–4 in 2004 (2.29) and 10–7 in 2005. His fifty-one starts are second all-time to Jered Weaver and his twenty-eight wins are third in the all-time list. Ramos was a starter for four years in the minors but has been stuck as a reliever in the majors, despite winning his first start, one of three in his career, in 2009. He's been in middle or situational relief ever since; in 2011, he pitched just less than an inning in fifty-nine games. He had a 2.10 ERA in seventeen appearances in 2012.

JEREMY REED / OF / 6-0, 195 / L-L
Born: June 15, 1981, San Dimas.
High School: Bonita.
College: Long Beach State.
Drafted: 2002, second round, Chicago White Sox.
Major League career: eight seasons (Seattle 2004–08, N.Y. Mets 2009, Toronto 2010, Milwaukee 2011).

Reed was a gamer who played good defense and hit .326 in his Dirtbag career with 135 runs scored, 110 RBI and fifty-four steals, second-most in school history. He got one extended look at the majors, with Seattle in 2005, and also played well for the Mets in 2009, but his lack of power kept him from becoming a day-to-day starter.

NIKCO RIESGO / OF / 6-2, 185 / R-R
Born: January 11, 1967, Long Beach.
High School: Poly
College: San Diego State.
Drafted: 1988, eighth round, San Diego.
Major League career: one season (Montreal 1991).

Riesgo had 104 stolen bases in his first three seasons in the minors but got into just four games with the Expos.

JACK ROTHROCK / OF-IF / 5-11, 165 / S-R
Born: March 14, 1905, Long Beach; Died: December 2, 1980.
High School: Poly.
Major League career: eleven seasons (Boston 1925–32, St. Louis 1934–35, Philadelphia A's 1937).

See chapter seven.

DON ROWE / P / 6-0, 180 / L-L
Born: April 3, 1936, Brawley, California; Died: October 15, 2005.
High School: Compton.
Major League career: one season (N.Y. Mets 1963).

Rowe was attending Compton College when he was signed in 1954, and he waited until 1963 for his one shot in the majors, when he had twenty-six appearances for the Mets. He coached at Compton College, Lynwood High and Pius X after his career. It took him thirteen years between his major and minor league stops to earn his degree from Long Beach State, and he was a baseball and football coach at Golden West College.

JACK SALVESON / P / 6-0, 180 / R-R
Born: January 5, 1914, Fullerton; Died: December 28, 1974.
High School: Poly.
College: Long Beach City College.
Major League career: five seasons (N.Y. Giants 1933–34; Pittsburgh 1935; Chicago White Sox 1935; Cleveland 1943, 1945).
See chapter thirteen.

PAUL SCHAAL / 3B / 5-11, 180 / R-R
Born: March 3, 1943, Pittsburgh, Pennsylvania.
High School: Compton.
Major League career: eleven seasons (L.A. Angels 1964–68, 1974; Kansas City 1969–74).

Schaal led Compton to a CIF title in 1961 and was signed by the Angels in their second year of existence. By 1965, he was their starting third baseman, hitting nine home runs. His best season was 1971 with the Royals when he hit eleven home runs, had sixty-three RBIs, hit .274 and walked 103 times.

GORDON SEYFRIED / P / 6-0, 185 / R-R
Born: July 4, 1937, Long Beach.
High School: Wilson.
Major League career: two seasons (Cleveland 1963–64).

Seyfried was a successful pitcher at Wilson who signed out of high school and won seventy-one games in a six-year span in the minors. He only made five appearances in the majors.

BRYAN SHAW / P / 6-1, 210 / R-R
Born: November 8, 1987, Livermore.
High School: Livermore.
College: Long Beach State.
Drafted: 2008, second round, Arizona.
Major League career: three seasons (Arizona 2011–12, Cleveland 2013).

Shaw was the 49ers closer for three seasons, going 9–5 with twenty-three saves in eighty games with a 2.20 career ERA. He led the team in ERA twice and in saves all three, topped by a 1.84 ERA and eleven in 2008. He stayed in the bullpen when Arizona signed him, and he had a 2.56 ERA in thirty-three appearances in 2011 and 3.49 in sixty-four in 2012. He was traded to Cleveland in the off-season.

DARRELL SHERMAN / OF / 5-9, 160 / L-L
Born: December 4, 1967, Los Angeles.
High School: Lynwood.
College: Cerritos College, Long Beach State.
Drafted: 1989, sixth round, San Diego.
Major League career: one season (San Diego 1993).

Sherman had success in high school and college and got a lot of attention with the original Dirtbags in 1989. In 1990, he had seventy-five steals in the minor leagues, but his progress stalled after thirty-seven games with the Padres in 1993. After being released at the end of 1995, he went on to play eleven more seasons in the Mexican League.

TOMMIE SISK / P / 6-3, 195 / R-R
Born: April 12, 1942, Ardmore, Oklahoma.
High School: Poly.
Major League career: nine seasons (Pittsburgh 1962–68, San Diego 1969, Chicago White Sox 1970).

Tommie Sisk, dining with Dodgers outfielder Willie Davis at a Long Beach Century Club banquet, was a lean right-hander with Poly who had a nine-year major league career.

Sisk's claim to baseball fame at Poly was being the winning pitcher in the first-ever game at Blair Field in 1958. But he also was an All-CIF basketball player in 1960 and helped lead the Jackrabbits to a CIF title. He was offered a basketball scholarship at UCLA by John Wooden. "I was always going to play baseball. By the time I was in the ninth grade, there were always scouts in the stands at my games. I loved baseball. It was what I always wanted to do," he said. He had a yeoman nine-season Major League career, spending seven of them with the Pirates. He made fifty-seven appearances in his second season with a 2.92 ERA, went 10–5 in 1966 and won a career-high thirteen games with eleven complete games in 1967. He won forty and saved ten games with a career 3.92 ERA.

Dave Skaugstad / P / 6-1, 179 / L-L
Born: January 10, 1940, Algona, Iowa.
High School: Compton.
Major League career: one season (Cincinnati 1957).

Skaugstad signed right off the Compton campus and made his Major League debut at the age of eighteen in 1957, making two appearances. He never got back to the majors.

Terrmel Sledge / OF / 6-0, 185 / L-L
Born: March 18, 1977, Fayetteville, North Carolina.
High School: Kennedy.
College: Cal State–Northridge, Long Beach State.
Drafted: 1999, eighth round, Seattle.
Major League career: four seasons (Montreal/Washington Nationals 2004–05, San Diego 2006–07).

Sledge transferred from Northridge when the Matadors dropped baseball before reversing its decision. Sledge made several all-time lists despite playing just two seasons: a .369 average (eighth), 171 runs (second) and twenty-two home runs (third). He scored ninety-nine runs in 1998, setting a single season record and fifteen more than No. 2. After hitting twenty-two home runs with ninety-two RBIs and a .342 average at Edmonton in 2003, he made the Expos starting lineup in 2004 and hit .269 with fifteen home runs and sixty-two RBIs. He had the last hit and RBI for the Montreal franchise before it moved to Washington, D.C.

BUD SMITH / P / 6-0, 170 / L-L
Born: October 23, 1979, Torrance.
High School: St. John Bosco (Bellflower).
College: L.A. Harbor.
Drafted: 1997, ninth round, Detroit.
Major League career: two seasons (St. Louis 2001–02).

He was 25–7 in a season-and-a-half in the minors before the Cardinals called him up in 2001. He went 6–3 and threw a no-hitter by the time 2001 was done but faded quickly in 2002 and spent just three more seasons in the farm system.

JIM SMITH / SS / 6-3, 185 / R-R
Born: September 8, 1954, Santa Monica.
High School: University (Waco, Texas).
College: El Camino, Long Beach State.
Drafted: 1976, sixth round, Baltimore.
Major League career: one season (Pittsburgh 1982).

Smith led the 49ers in hits, runs, doubles and RBIs in 1974 and was a three-year letterman. He waded through six years in the farm system before Pittsburgh gave him a shot, getting forty-two at-bats in 1982.

DUKE SNIDER / OF / 6-0, 190 / L-R
Born: September 9, 1926, Los Angeles. Died: February 27, 2011.
High School: Compton.
Major League career: eighteen seasons (Brooklyn/L.A. Dodgers 1947–62, N.Y. Mets 1963, San Francisco Giants 1964).

See chapter four.

VERN STEPHENS / SS / 5-10, 185 / R-R
Born: October 23, 1920, McAlister, New Mexico; Died: October 3, 1968.
High School: Poly.
College: Long Beach City College.
Major League career: fifteen seasons (St. Louis Browns 1941–47, 1953; Boston Red Sox 1948–52, Chicago White Sox 1953, 1955; Baltimore Orioles 1954–55).

See chapter six.

CHUCK STEVENS / 1B / 6-1, 180 / S-L
Born: July 10, 1918, Van Houton, New Mexico.
High School: Poly.
Major League career: three seasons (St. Louis Browns 1941, 1946, 1948).
See chapter thirteen.

LEE STINE / P / 5-11, 185 / R-R
Born: November 17, 1913, Stillwater, Oklahoma; Died: May 6, 2005
High school: Poly.
Major League career: four seasons (Chicago White Sox 1934–35, Cincinnati 1936, N.Y. Yankees 1938).

Those who saw Stine pitch in youth ball raved about his talent and speed, and he was pitching in PCL by the time he was sixteen. He suffered an arm injury early in his career that set him back, but he still reached the majors and in 1936 appeared in 40 games with the Reds. He won 111 games between 1933 and 1941 in the minors.

GEORGE STOVALL / 1B / 6-2, 180 / R-R
Born: November 23, 1977, Leeds, Missouri; Died, November 5, 1951
High School: Poly.
Major League career: twelve seasons (Cleveland 1904–11, St. Louis Browns 1912–13, Kansas City Packers 1914–15; Federal League).

Stovall's link to Poly is tenuous. He was living in Long Beach and played in one game for Poly when he was twenty-two. This was the era before high school sports were organized and had things like eligibility rules. But he did spend time here with his brother Jesse during the off-seasons and had an interesting life and career, spending his last two Major League seasons in the outlaw Federal League, managing the Vernon PCL team in 1917, coaching at Loyola Marymount, running a semipro league in Long Beach and working in the shipyards in both World Wars.

JIM STRICKLAND / P / 6-0, 175 / L-L
Born: June 12, 1948, Los Angeles.
High School: Lakewood.
Major League career: four seasons (Minnesota 1971–73, Cleveland 1975).

Strickland signed with the Dodgers out of high school and might have had a different career if he hadn't spent two years serving in Vietnam (1967–68). He was signed by Tommy Lasorda and made sixty appearances in relief in his four seasons as a lefty specialist, posting a 2.68 in sixty games and seventy-seven and one-third innings.

Bobby Sturgeon (Poly) was a superb infielder who had an eight-year major league career, finishing it with the Boston Braves.

BOBBY STURGEON / SS / 6-0, 175 / R-R
Born: August 6, 1919, Clinton, Indiana; Died, March 10, 2007.
High School: Poly.
Major League career: six seasons (Chicago Cubs 1940–42, 1946–57; BostonV Braves 1948).

Sturgeon is one of the many what-ifs to come out of World War II. He was the Cubs starting second baseman in 1941 but lost three years to the military (1943–45). He was stationed locally and played on several barnstorming and winter teams while in the service. He regained his starting job in 1946 and hit .296, but his Major League career faded thereafter. He got into thirty-four games for the N.L. Champion Boston Braves in his final season in 1948. He played in the PCL after his Major League days and spent five years as a minor league manager before retiring and serving Long Beach in the recreation department and working for Douglas aerospace.

CRAIG SWAN / P / 6-3, 215 / R-R
Born: November 30, 1950, Van Nuys.
High School: Millikan.
College: Arizona State.
Drafted: 1972, third round, N.Y. Mets.
Major League career: twelve seasons (N.Y. Mets 1973–84, L.A. Angels 1984).

Swan led Millikan to the 1967 CIF title and went to Arizona State during its glory years. In 1972, he allowed one run in eighteen innings pitched at the College World Series to tie a CWS record. He reacheVd the majors after being named the International League's most valuable pitcher in 1975 and made the Mets rotation in 1976 while posting a 3.54 ERA. In '78 and '79, he was the star on otherwise miserable Mets teams. In 1978, he led the N.L. in ERA (2.43) but had just a 9–6 record in twenty-eight starts. Ditto for '79, when the Mets lost ninety-nine games but Swan was 14–13. Injuries scuttled the rest of his career.

ZEB TERRY / SS-2B / 5-8, 129 / R-R
Born: June 17, 1891, Denison, Texas; Died: March 14, 1988.
High School: Poly.
College: Stanford.
Major League career: seven seasons (Chicago White Sox 1916–17, Boston Braves 1918, Pittsburgh 1919, Chicago Cubs 1920–22).

Baseball-Reference.com claims Terry graduated from Poly. He would have graduated in 1910, and there's no records verifying he played baseball at Poly. He played at Stanford before a six-year career that included four seasons as a starter, hitting .275 or better in three of them. He also played four seasons with the PCL's L.A. Angels.

GEORGE THROOP / P / 6-7, 205 / R-R
Born: November 24, 1950, Pasadena.
High School: Pasadena.
College: Pasadena Community College, Long Beach State.
Drafted: 1972, sixteenth round, Kansas City.
Major League career: four seasons (Kansas City 1975, 1977–79; Houston 1979).

Throop led the 49ers in ERA at 2.12 in his lone season of 1972. He reached the majors in four years, but he didn't get many opportunities. He appeared in fourteen games for the Astros in 1979 with a win and 3.72 ERA.

STEVE TRACHSEL / P / 6-3, 185 / R-R
Born: October 31, 1970, Oxnard.
High School: Troy.
College: Fullerton College, Long Beach State.
Drafted: 1991, eighth round, Chicago Cubs.
Major League career: sixteen seasons (Chicago Cubs 1993–99, 2008; Tampa 2000; Toronto 2000; N.Y. Mets 2001–06; Baltimore 2007–08).

Trachsel helped lead the Dirtbags to the 1991 CWS, going 11–6 with a 2.78 ERA and school record 148 $^{1}/_{3}$ innings. He was an inning-eater in his long pro career, making twenty-eight to thirty-three starts a year from 1995 to 2004 and threw 200-plus innings seven times. He had his best seasons with the Mets, winning sixty-six games with a 4.09 ERA. He made the 1996 All-Star game and gave up Mark McGwire's record-breaking sixty-second home run in 1998.

TROY TULOWITZKI / SS / 6-3, 215 / R-R
Born: October 10, 1984, Santa Clara.
High School: Fremont (Sunnyvale).
College: Long Beach State.
Drafted: 2005, first round, Colorado.
Major League career: eight seasons (Colorado 2006–2013).
See chapter eleven.

BRIAN TURANG / OF / 5-10, 170 / R-R
Born: June 14, 1967, Long Beach.
High School: Millikan.
College: Long Beach City College, Loyola Marymount.
Drafted: 1989, fifty-first round, Seattle.
Major League career: two seasons (Seattle 1993–94).

The small outfielder hustled his way into a brief pro career, going from a low-round pick to eight pro seasons including two brief stops with the Mariners.

TOM URBANI / P / 5-1, 190 / L-L
Born: January 21, 1968, Santa Cruz.
High School: Harbor (Santa Cruz).
College: Cabrillo, Long Beach State.
Drafted: 1990, thirteenth round, St. Louis.
Major League career: four seasons (St. Louis 1993–96, Detroit 1996).

Urbani spent two years with the 49ers, filling both starting and relief roles. He had a 3.70 as a swingman in 1995. After his Major League career ended, he played professionally for Remini in Italy and won twelve games with a 1.35 ERA and a perfect game in 1999. The same year, he played for the national team that won the silver medal at the European Championships.

CHASE UTLEY / 2B / 6-1, 185 / R-R
Born: December 17, 1978, Pasadena.
High School: Poly.
College: UCLA.
Drafted: 2000, first round, Philadelphia.
Major League career: eleven seasons (Philadelphia 2003–2013).

No one who saw Utley as a youngster could have predicted he would become a slugger for the Philadelphia Phillies. The second baseman played in the same Little League as the kids who were on the 1992 and 1993 Long

Beach Little League World Champions. "He could hit drives in the gaps and run with abandon," Jeff Burroughs, the former Wilson standout and 1974 A.L. MVP who coached those two teams, said. "But he was also the runt of the league. He was a good athlete who could have played most anything. He was a very good soccer player, and he had coaches telling him to focus on soccer. But all he ever really wanted to do was play baseball." Even in his first two seasons at Poly, he was still considered thin and weak-armed. He was cut from a pro scout team the fall before his junior season and then was passed over for the annual showcase scouting event, the Area Code Games, held at Blair Field. Then he grew a few inches, added a few pounds and his senior season arrived. Utley began clubbing home runs, a Moore League–record twelve in all. He hit three in the same week at Blair Field and set a state record with a home run in six consecutive games. Utley starred at UCLA, hitting 15 home runs as a freshman. By the end of his junior season, he had compiled a career .342 average and 53 home runs. The Phillies made him the fifteenth pick in the first round of the 2000 draft. Utley made it to the Phillies full-time in 2005 and over the next five years put up stunning statistics for a second baseman—146 home runs, 507 RBI, an average over .300, four Silver Slugger awards and topping the leaderboard in putouts and assists defensively several times. He was the MVP of the Phils' 2008 World Series champs and in 2009 hit 5 home runs in the series against the Yankees. Knee injuries limited him to 301 games from 2010 to 2012.

JASON VARGAS / P / 6-0, 215 / L-L
Born: February 2, 1983, Apple Valley.
High School: Apple Valley.
College: LSU, Cypress, Long Beach State.
Drafted: 2004, second round, Florida.
Major League career: seven seasons (Florida 2005–06, N.Y. Mets 2007, Seattle 2009–12, L.A. Angels 2013).

Vargas began his career at LSU but chose to return home after a year and earned SoCal player of the year honors at Cypress. He was signed by Long Beach and was a two-way star in 2004, filling the No. 3 slot in the rotation (7–6, 4.14) and leading the team in average (.354), hits and runs as a first-baseman/DH. He made a quick jump to the majors in 2005, going 5–5 with a 4.03 ERA. He was traded to the Mets, and he had elbow issues during the season and then in the off-season underwent surgery for a tear in his hip and missed all of 2008. Everything matured in 2010, and over the next three seasons, he made ninety-six starts (thirty-three wins) with a sub-4.00 ERA and low walk rate for a bad Seattle franchise. He was traded to the Angels for 2013 and rejoined Jered Weaver, who was his teammate in 2004.

Nick Vincent / P / 6-0, 185 / R-R
Born: July 12, 1986, Poway.
High School: Ramona.
College: Palomar, Long Beach State.
Drafted: 2008, eighteenth round, San Diego.
Major League career: one season (San Diego 2012).

Vincent was the heir to the closer role vacated by Shaw, but he did so well in his middle relief efforts—twenty-six games, team-leading 1.76 ERA, two saves—that San Diego drafted him low but offered a decent bonus, and he chose to sign. He was 2–0 in twenty-six innings with a 1.71 ERA in 2012 but opened 2013 in the minors.

Reggie Walton / OF / 6-3, 205 / R-R
Born: October 24, 1952, Kansas City, Missouri.
High School: Compton.
College: Compton College.
Drafted: 1972, second round, San Francisco.
Major League career: three seasons (Seattle 1980–81, Pittsburgh 1982).

Walton hit over .300 in three of five minor league seasons with the Giants but never got a call-up, so he played in the Mexican League for two seasons (1977–78) before returning to the United States, finally getting a chance with Seattle at the age of twenty-seven. He hit .277 in a brief stint with the Mariners in 1980.

Gary Ward / OF / 6-2, 202 / R-R
Born: December 6, 1953, Los Angeles.
High School: Compton.
Major League career: twelve seasons (Minnesota 1979–83, Texas 1984–86, N.Y. Yankees 1987–89, Detroit 1989–90).

Ward had a quite good career after being signed as an undrafted free agent, blossoming with the Twins in 1982 when he had 28 home runs, ninety-one RBIs and hit .289. He hit for the cycle in a 1980 game and was a two-time All-Star. In 1984, he hit 21 home runs for Texas and retired with a career .276 average and 130 home runs. He's the father of former Dodger Daryle Ward.

BOB WATKINS / P / 6-0, 170 / R-R
Born: March 17, 1948, San Francisco.
High School: Compton.
Drafted: 1966, twenty-second round, Houston.
Major League career: one season (Houston 1969).

Watkins pitched in five games with the Astros in 1969.

JERED WEAVER / P / 6-7, 210 / R-R
Born: October 4, 1982, Northridge.
High School: Simi Valley.
College: Long Beach State.
Drafted: 2004, first round, L.A. Angels.
Major League career: eight seasons (L.A. Angels 2006–13).

See chapter eleven.

ADAM WILK / P / 6-2, 180 / L-L
Born: December 9, 1987, Anaheim.
High School: Cypress.
College: Long Beach State.
Drafted: 2009, eleventh round, Detroit.
Major League career: two seasons (Detroit 2011–12).

Wilk went from reliever to starter in his three-year career, going 10–4 in fifty-two games with sixteen saves and a 3.04 ERA. He made a rapid rise in the Tigers organization and got into five games in 2011, then made three starts in 2012 and was sent back to the minors. He was 26–22 from 2010–12 for the Tigers' Toledo franchise with an ERA around 3.00. He asked for his release after 2012 so he could play for a team in Korea in 2013 with an eye on returning to the majors.

CHARLIE WILLIAMS / Umpire
Born: December 20, 1943, Denver; Died, September 10, 2005.
High school: Poly.
College: Long Beach City College, Cal State–L.A.
Major League career: 18 seasons (1982–2000).

Williams played football and baseball at Poly and LBCC but wasn't thinking of officiating until a friend told him about an umpire training camp in 1974. Within a year, Williams was umpiring in the minors and joined MLB in 1982. He was the first African American to work home plate in a World Series game, the wild Game 4 of the 1993 series, won by Toronto 15–14. It was the longest series game on record.

Bill Wilson began his career at Jordan as an ace infielder before moving to the outfield as a pro. He hit 17 home runs in 1954 and 15 in 1955 before finishing his minor league career with 228 home runs. He's shown sliding here in a shot from his American Legion days with a team from Anaheim.

BILL WILSON / OF / 6-2, 220 / R-R
Born: November 6, 1928, Central City, Nebraska.
High School: Jordan.
Major League career: four seasons (Chicago White Sox 1950, 1953–54; Philadelphia A's/K.C. A's 1954–55).

Wilson was an under-appreciated power hitter and good fielder who showed his power twice in the majors but didn't stick, hitting 17 home runs in 1954 and 1955. He hit 36 for Memphis in the minors in 1950, missed two seasons in the military and hit 30 when he came back in 1953. He hit 228 home runs in just 1,315 minor league games, an average of a home run every nineteen at-bats.

VANCE WORLEY / P / 6-2, 230 / R-R
Born: September 25, 1987, Sacramento.

High School: McClatchy.
College: Long Beach State.
Drafted: 2008, third round, Philadelphia.
Major League career: four seasons (Philadelphia 2010–12, Minnesota 2013.

Worley arrived in Long Beach a prized recruit, but he had injury issues his entire career, going 12–13 in forty-seven games (thirty-two starts, fifteen in relief).

He was 4–7 in a split role as a freshman, missed most of his sophomore season to injury and was moved to bullpen as a junior to reduce stress on his arm. His talent was visible nonetheless, and he was good enough to be a third-round pick in 2008. He paid off in 2011 when he was 11–3 with a 3.01 ERA when he replaced an injured Joe Blanton in the rotation. He tailed off to 6–9 in 2012 and was traded to Minnesota in off-season.

The original scope of the book was to include bios on all of the players who reached the majors from theses area schools, but space caused a casualty. A list of the high schools and their Major Leaguers:

Artesia Pioneers (three): Dick Wantz, P, one season (L.A. Angels 1965); **Ed Hodge**, C, one season (Minnesota 1984); **Joel Adamson,** P, three seasons (Minnesota 1996–98).

Bellflower Buccaneers (five): Bob Lee, P, five seasons (L.A. Angels 1964–66, L.A. Dodgers 1967, Cincinnati 1967–68). **Steve Staggs**, OF, two seasons (Kansas City 1977–78); **Eric Plunk**, P, fourteen seasons (Oakland 1986–89, N.Y. Yankees 1989–91, Cleveland 1992–98, Milwaukee 1998–99); **Mike Benjamin**, IF, thirteen seasons (San Francisco 1989–95, Philadelphia 1976, Boston 1997–98, Pittsburgh 1999–2000, 2002); **Anthony Gose**, OF, two seasons (Toronto 2012-13).

Centennial Apaches (ten): Roy White, OF, fifteen seasons (N.Y. Yankees 1965–79). **Reggie Smith**, OF, seventeen seasons (Boston 1966–1973, St. Louis 1974–76, L.A. Dodgers 1976–81, San Francisco 1982); **Don Wilson**, P, nine seasons (Houston 1966–74); **Wayne Simpson**, P, six seasons (Cincinnati 1970–72, Kansas City 1973, Philadelphia 1975, L.A. Angels 1977); **Lenny Randle**, IF, twelve seasons (Washington/Texas 1971–76, N.Y. Mets 1977–78, N.Y. Yankees 1979, Chicago Cubs 1980, Seattle 1981–82); **Al Cowens**, OF, thirteen seasons (Kansas City 1974–79, L.A. Angels 1980, Detroit 1980–81, Seattle 1982–86); **John Scott**, three seasons (San Diego 1974–75, Toronto 1977); **Mitchell Page**, OF-DH, eight seasons (Oakland 1977–83, Pittsburgh 1984); **Lonnie Smith**, OF, seventeen seasons (Philadelphia 1978–81, St. Louis 1982–85, Kansas City

1985–87, Atlanta 1988–92, Pittsburgh 1993, Baltimore 1993–94); **George Hinshaw**, two seasons (San Diego, 1982–83).

Cerritos Dons (two): Jeff Hearron, C, two seasons (Toronto, 1985–86); **Rickey Cradle**, OF, one season (Seattle 1998).

Cerritos Valley Christian Crusaders (two): John Verhoeven, P, four seasons (L.A. Angels 1976–77, Chicago White Sox 1977, Minnesota 1980–81). **Kirk Saarloos**, P, seven seasons (Houston 2002–03, Oakland 2004–06, 2008, Cincinnati 2007).

Dominguez Dons (four): Eric Raich, P, two seasons (Cleveland 1975–76); **Ken Landreaux**, OF, eleven seasons (L.A. Angels 1977–78, Minnesota 1979–80), L.A. Dodgers (1981–87); **Rick Peters**, five seasons (Detroit 1979–81, Oakland 1983, 1986); **Hubie Brooks**, IF, fifteen seasons (N.Y. Mets 1980–84, 1991; Montreal 1985–89; L.A. Dodgers 1990; L.A. Angels 1992; Kansas City 1993–94).

Downey Vikings (one): Rube Ellis, P, four seasons (St. Louis, 1909–12).

Gahr Gladiators (eight): Dan Boone, P, three seasons (San Diego 1981–82, Houston 1982, Baltimore 1990); **Tom Nieto**, C, seven seasons (St. Louis 1984–85, Montreal 1986, Minnesota 1987–88, Philadelphia 1989–90); **Shane Mack**, OF, nine seasons (San Diego 1987–88, Minnesota 1990–94, Boston 1997, Oakland 1998, Kansas City 1998); **Al Osuna**, P, six seasons (Houston 1990–93, L.A Dodgers 1994, San Diego 1996); **Bret Barberie**, IF, six seasons (Montreal 1991–92, Florida 1993–94, Baltimore 1995, Chicago Cubs 1996); **Quinn Mack**, OF, one season (Seattle 1994); **Val Pascucci**, two seasons (Montreal 2004, N.Y. Mets 2011); **Kris Medlen**, five seasons (Atlanta 2009–13).

John Glenn Eagles (one): Tommy Moore, four seasons (N.Y. Mets 1972–73, St. Louis 1975, Texas 1975, Seattle 1977).

Los Alamitos Griffins (seven): Craig Chamberlain, **Greg Harris**, see registry; **J.T. Snow**, 1B, fifteen seasons (N.Y. Yankees 1992; L.A. Angels 1993–96; San Francisco 1997–2005, 2008); **Robb Nen**, P, ten seasons (Texas 1993, Florida 1993–97, San Francisco 1998–2002). **Greg Pirkl**, 1B, four seasons (Seattle 1993–96, Boston 1996); **Mike Kelly**, OF, six years (Atlanta 1994–95, Cincinnati 1996–97, Tampa 1998, Colorado 1999); **Chase D'Arnaud**, SS, Three seasons (Pittsburgh 2011–13).

Lynwood Knights (nine): Rod Miller, OF, one season (Brooklyn 1957); **Mike Kekich**, P, nine seasons (L.A. Dodgers 1965, 1968; N.Y. Yankees 1969–73; Cleveland 1973; Texas 1975; Seattle 1977); **Don Carrithers**, P, eight seasons (San Francisco 1970–73, Montreal 1974–76, Minnesota 1977); **Jim Barr**, P, twelve seasons (San Francisco 1971–80,

L.A. Angels 1982–83); **John Fuller**, one season (Atlanta 1974); **Lorenzo Gray**, two seasons (White Sox 1982–83); **Jessie Reid**, two seasons (San Francisco 1987–88); **Darrell Sherman**, see registry; **Efran Navarro**, 1B, one season (L.A. Angels 2011).

Mayfair Monsoons (two): Jay Gibbons, OF, nine seasons (Baltimore 2001–07, L.A. Dodgers 2010–11). **Justin Turner**, 2B, five seasons (N.Y. Mets 2009–13).

Neff Trojans (one): Jerry Maddox, one season (Atlanta 1978).

Norwalk Lancers (four): Lee Bales, two seasons (Atlanta 1966, Houston 1967); **Jim York**, P, seven seasons (Kansas City 1970–71, Houston 1972–75, N.Y. Yankees 1976); **Mark Portugal**, P, fifteen seasons (Minnesota 1985–88, Houston 1989–93, San Francisco 1994–95, Cincinnati 1995–99, Philadelphia 1997–98, Boston 1999). **Larry See**, 1B, two seasons (L.A. Dodgers 1986, Texas 1988).

Paramount Pirates (three): Jeff Sellers, four seasons (Boston 1985–88); **Brian Hunter**, OF, nine seasons (Atlanta 1991–93, 1999–2000, Pittsburgh 1994, Cincinnati 1994–95, Seattle 1996, St. Louis 1998, Philadelphia 2000); **Gil Velazquez**, IF four seasons (Boston 2008–09, L.A. Angels 2011, Miami 2012).

Pius X Warriors (two): Mike Paul, P, seven seasons (Cleveland 1968–71, Texas 1972–73, Chicago Cubs 1973–74); **Augie Ojeda**, IF, nine seasons (Chicago Cubs 2000–03, Minnesota 2004, Arizona 2007–10).

Warren Bears (four): Bob Apodaca, P, five seasons (N.Y. Mets 1973–77); R**ick Burleson**, SS, thirteen seasons (Boston 1974–80, L.A. Angels 1981–94, 1996).; **Luis Medina**, three seasons (Cleveland 1988–89, 1991); **Bobby LaFromboise**, P, one season (Seattle 2013).

Cal State–Dominguez Hills Toros (five): LaRue Washington, two seasons (Texas 1978–79); **George Stablein**, 1B, one season (San Diego 1980); **DeWayne Buice**, P, three seasons (L.A. Angels 1987–88, Toronto 1989); **Craig Grebeck**, see registry; **Jim Pena,** one season (San Francisco 1992).

Cerritos College (twenty-nine): Dick Wantz, **Ed Hodge**, **Joel Adamson**, see Artesia; **Steve Staggs**, **Mike Benjamin**, see Bellflower; **Lee Bales, Jim York, Larry See**, see Norwalk, **Mike Paul**, see Pius X; **Tommy Moore**, see Glenn; **Bob Apodaca, Luis Medina**, see Warren; **Jerry Maddox**, see Neff; **Dan Boone**, **Tom Nieto**, **Bret Barbarie**, **Al Osuna**, **Quinn Mack**, see Gahr; **Jerry Hearron**, see Cerritos; **Jessie Reid**, see Lynwood; **Brian Hunter**, see Paramount; **Darrell Sherman**, see registry; **Dave Patterson**, P, one season (L.A. Dodgers 1979); **Craig**

Worthington, IF, seven seasons (Baltimore 1988–91, Cleveland 1992, Cincinnati 1995, Texas 1995–96); **Ever Magallanes**, one season (Cleveland 1991); **Dan Naulty**, P, four seasons (Minnesota 1996–98, N.Y. Yankees 1999); **Dusty Wathan**, C, one season (Kansas City, 2002); **Dan Patterson**, P, nine seasons (Texas 1996–99, Detroit 2000–04); **Rod Barajas**, **C**, fourteen seasons (Arizona 1999–2003, Texas 2004–06, Philadelphia 2007, Toronto 2008–09, N.Y. Mets 2010, L.A. Dodgers 2010–11, Pittsburgh 2012.

Compton College (seven): Don Wilson, **Mitchell Page**, see Centennial; **Odell Jones**, **Reggie Walton**, **Oscar Brown**, **Jim Marshall**, see registry; **Dave Nelson**, IF, ten seasons (Cleveland 1968–69, Washington/Texas 1970–75, Kansas City 1976–77).

The following players were born in Greater Long Beach but did not attend area high schools or colleges: **Chris Arnold** (LB), IF, six seasons (San Francisco 1971–76); **Alan Ashby** (LB), C, seventeen seasons (Cleveland 1973–76, Toronto 1977–78, Houston 1979–89); **Jason Bates** (Downey), OF, four seasons (Colorado 1995–98); **Bill Bathe** (Downey), three seasons (Oakland 1986, San Francisco 1989–1990); **Brant Billingsley** (Downey), P, one Season (Florida 1999); **Ben Blomdahl** (LB), OF, one Season (Detroit 1995); **Derek Botelho** (LB), P, two seasons (Kansas City 1982, Chicago Cubs 1985; **Justin Brunette** (Los Alamitos), P, one season (St. Louis 2000); **Gary Buckels** (La Mirada), P, one season (St. Louis 1994); **Bud Bulling** (Lynwood), C, four seasons (Minnesota 1977, Seattle 1981–83); **Marty Castillo** (LB), 3B-C, five seasons (Detroit, 1981–85); **Joe Christensen** (Downey), OF, four seasons (N.Y. Mets 1984–85, Seattle 1987, Minnesota 1988); **Gary Cooper** (Lynwood), 3B, one season (Houston 1991); **Khris Davis** (Lakewood), OF, one season (Milwaukee 2013)**; Jim Derrington** (Compton), P, two seasons (Chicago White Sox, 1956–57); **Scott Erickson** (LB), P, fifteen seasons (Minnesota 1990–95, Baltimore 1995–2000, 2002, N.Y. Mets 2004, Texas 2004, L.A. Dodgers 2005, New York Yankees 2006); **Randy Flores** (Bellflower), P, eight seasons (Texas 2002, Colorado 2002, 2009–10), St. Louis 2004–08, Minnesota 2010); **Mike Fyhrie** (LB), P, five seasons (N.Y. Mets 1996, L.A. Angels 1999–2000, Chicago Cubs 2001, Oakland 2001–02); **Chris Gardner** (LB), P, one season (Houston 1991); **Cole Garner** (LB), OF, one season (Colorado 2011). **Brian Greer** (Lynwood), OF, two seasons (San Diego, 1977, 1979); **Keith Ginter** (Norwalk), 2B, six seasons (Houston 2000–02, Milwaukee 2002–04, Oakland 2005); **Kevin Gross** (Downey), P, fifteen seasons (Philadelphia 1983–88, Montreal 1989–90, L.A. Dodgers 1991–94, Texas 1995–96, L.A. Angels 1997); **Anthony Gwynn** (LB), OF, seven seasons (Milwaukee 2006–08, San Diego 2009–10, L.A. Dodgers 2011–12); **Greg Hansell** (Bellflower), P, four seasons (L.A. Dodgers 1995, Minnesota 1996, Milwaukee 1997, Pittsburgh 1999); **Dave Hansen** (LB), 3B-PH, fifteen seasons (L.A. Dodgers 1990–96, 1999–2002, Cleveland 1997, San Diego 2003–04, Seattle 2004–05); **Gary Holman** (LB), 1B, two seasons (Washington 1968–69); **John Harrell** (LB), C, one season (San Francisco 1969); **Bill Henry** (LB), P, one season (N.Y. Yankees 1966).

Trevor Hoffman (Bellflower), P, eighteen seasons (Florida 1993, San Diego 1993–2008, Milwaukee 2009–10); **Tyler Houston** (LB), 3B-C, eight seasons (Atlanta 1996, Chicago Cubs 1996–99, Cleveland 1999, Milwaukee 2000–02, L.A. Dodgers 2002, Philadelphia 2003); **Ron Johnson** (LB), 1B, three seasons (Kansas City 1982–83, Montreal 1984); **Carl Jones** (Compton), P, two seasons (Seattle 1991–92); **Jeff Kent** (Bellflower), 2B, seventeen seasons (Toronto 1992, N.Y. Mets 1992–96, Cleveland 1996, San Francisco 1997–2002, Houston 2003-04), L.A. Dodgers 2005-08); **Mike Krukow** (LB), P, 14 seasons (Chicago Cubs 1976-81, Philadelphia 1982, San Francisco 1983–89); **Matt Luke** (LB), OF, three seasons (N.Y. Yankees 1996, L.A. Dodgers 1998, Cleveland 1998, L.A. Angels 1999); **Ryan Madson** (LB), P, ten seasons (Philadelphia 2003–11, L.A. Angels 2013); **Donzell McDonald** (LB), OF, two seasons (N.Y. Yankees 2001, Kansas City 2002); **Ryan McGuire** (Bellflower), 1B, six seasons (Montreal 1997–99, N.Y. Mets 2000, Florida 2001, Boston 2002); **Mike Misuraca** (LB), P, one season (Milwaukee 1997).

Scott Moore (LB), IF, five seasons (Chicago Cubs 2006–07, Baltimore 2007–08, 2010, Houston 2012); **Sean Mulligan** (Lynwood), OF, one season (San Diego 1996); **Dan Murphy** (Artesia), P, one season (San Diego 1989); **Donny Murphy** (Lakewood), IF, six seasons (Kansas City 2004–05, Oakland 2007–08, Florida 2010–11); **Dan Murray** (Los Alamitos), P, two seasons (N.Y. Mets 1999, Kansas City 1999–2000); **Rob Natal** (LB), C, six seasons (Montreal 1992, Florida 1993–97); **Troy O'Leary** (Compton), OF, eleven seasons (Milwaukee 1993–94, Boston 1995–2001, Montreal 2002, Cleveland 2003); **Dennis Paepke** (LB), C, four seasons (1969, 1971–72, 1974); **Craig Paquette** (LB), 3B-Of, eleven seasons (Oakland 92–95, Kansas City 1996–97, N.Y. Mets 1998, St. Louis 1999–2001, Detroit 2002–03); **Chris Parmelee** (LB), 1B-OF, three seasons (Minnesota 2011–13); **Jim Parque** (Norwalk), P, six seasons (Chicago White Sox 1998–2002, Tampa 2003); **Adam Peterson** (LB), P, five seasons (Chicago White Sox 1987–90, San Diego 1991); **Jeremy Powell** (La Mirada), P, three seasons (Montreal 1998–2000); **Brian Puffer** (Downey), P, four seasons (Houston

2002–04, San Francisco 2005); **Carlos Quentin** (Bellflower), OF, eight seasons (Arizona 2006–07, Chicago White Sox 2008–11, San Diego 2012–13); **Mark Quinn** (La Mirada), OF, four seasons (Kansas City 1999–2002); **Anthony Reyes** (Downey), P, five seasons (St. Louis 2005–08, Chicago Cubs 2008–09); **Rich Rodriguez** (Downey), P, thirteen seasons (San Diego 1990–93, Florida 1994, St. Louis 1994–95, San Francisco 1997–99, N.Y. Mets 2000, Cleveland 2001, Texas 2002, L.A. Angels 2003); **Ed Sukla** (LB), P, three seasons (L.A. Angels 1964–66); **Ian Stewart** (LB), IF, six seasons (Colorado 2007–11, Chicago Cubs 2012).

Tim Salmon (LB), OF, fourteen seasons (L.A. Angels 1992–2004, 2006); **Sergio Santos** (Bellflower), P, three seasons (Chicago White Sox 2010–11, Toronto 2012–13); **Rich Severson** (Artesia), IF, two seasons (Kansas City 1970–71); **Jim Slaton** (LB), P, sixteen seasons (Milwaukee 1971–77, 1979–83, Detroit 1978, 1986, L.A. Angels 1984–86); **Don Slaught** (LB), C, sixteen seasons (Kansas City 1982–84, Texas 1985–87, N.Y. Yankees 1988–89, Pittsburgh 1990–95, L.A. Angels 1996, Cleveland 1996, San Diego 1997); **Steve Springer** (LB), 3B, two seasons (Cleveland 1990, N.Y. Yankees 1992); **Eric Valent** (La Mirada), OF, five seasons (Philadelphia 2001–02, Cincinnati 2003, N.Y. Mets 2004–05); **Gene Vaughan** (Compton), OF, one season (Houston 1963); **Daryle Ward** (Lynwood), OF, eleven seasons (Houston 1998–2002, Pittsburgh 2004–05, L.A. Dodgers 2006, Atlanta 2007, Cleveland 2007–08); **Curt Wardle** (Downey), P, two seasons (Minnesota 1984–85, Cleveland 1985); **Myron White** (LB), OF, one season (Dodgers 1978); **George Witt** (LB), P, six seasons (Pittsburgh 1957–61, L.A. Angels 1962, Houston 1962).

INDEX

C

D

E

F

G

H

I

J

K

L

M

Q

R

S

T

U

V

W

Y

ABOUT THE AUTHOR

Bob Keisser has been a sportswriter in Southern California his entire life, starting at the *Los Angeles Herald Examiner* in 1973 and staying in the respected and feisty sports section until the paper's demise in 1989. In 1990, he joined the staff of the *Long Beach Press-Telegram*, initially serving as beat writer for the L.A. Raiders before becoming a columnist and features writer.

He is a graduate of Los Angeles City College and Cal State–Los Angeles with degrees in journalism. He lives in Long Beach and has a son who is a junior at Long Beach State.